Look up

For Your Redemption Is Near

Look Up For Your Redemption Is Near

Copyright © 2008, John M. Mendola

ISBN (Paperback): 978-1-916849-99-0

ISBN (Hardcover): 978-1-917184-00-7

Psalms for the World, Inc.

30025 Alicia Parkway, Unit 192

Laguna Niguel, CA 92677

TEL: 949-565-1050

Jmendola62@gmail.com

WeChat: drjohnnyrock

Psalms For The World, Inc.

An International Bible Teaching Ministry

T a b l e   o f
C o n t e n t s

FOREWARD

Many Bible students find the study of biblical prophecy confusing.

My practice when approaching a subject that I know little about is to find the simplest thing written on it. Then I move on to something a little more difficult and then to something more difficult still.

John Mendola has produced an easy-to-understand summary of key areas in the study of what the Bible has to say about future things. Digesting these studies will prepare the way for deeper work in these areas. I recommend his writings as a great place to lay a foundation.

Pastor Carl Westerlund

Director / Calvary Chapel Costa Mesa School Of Ministry

Carl Westerlund has been in pastoral ministry since 1968. He has been on the staff at Calvary Chapel Costa Mesa since 1987. He directs the School of Ministry, which is an alternative seminary program.

ACKNOWLEDGMENTS

Romans 8:28 states, "And we know that all things work together for good to them that love God, to them who are the called according to his purpose."

For that reason, I would like to thank my Lord and Savior, Jesus Christ, for calling me to write these lessons for you. I thank my mom and dad for their prayers that kept me alive through my teens; my sister, Donna, and her husband, Whitey, for all their help; Evangeline, my wonderful wife, for being grounded in the Word and supporting my long hours of study; my two sons, Joshua and Caleb, for allowing me to experience the true love that a father has for his sons. Thanks to my pastor, Chuck Smith, of Calvary Chapel of Costa Mesa, California, for his anointed, sound, biblical teaching; Pastor Carl Westerlund for always being there; all of our friends at Calvary Chapel Monday night Bible study; the Harvest Praise Band for their encouragement; the sisters in daycare for all of their love and patience for the children; Greg Laurie for his powerful messages; Cathe Laurie for her inspiration; the late Tara Inouye for all her hours donated to the ministry; Greg Dowd for being a great friend; Tom and LaDonna Jaso for their years of prayers and support; Israel K. and all of the brothers and sisters at Psalms for the World India for their intercessory prayer; Earl Williams at IBI Bible College for his support with our India project; and David, Latisha, and Lukas for their friendship, love, and help.

INTRODUCTION

With the hustle and bustle of today's schedules and demands, it is extremely hard to stay focused on things that matter. Can you imagine yourself being Moses? After a traumatic beginning of being hidden and away from his loving family, then being found and adopted by royalty, raised by royalty with all its privileges, only to end up running away into the desert and spending forty years there, then another forty years out in the wilderness. Talk about an oxymoron—royalty to poverty, feast to famine.

God asked him to become a leader, and even with all of his education and privilege, he felt inadequate and gave God an excuse. He finally became a leader and followed God's plan for the Children of Israel. He walked close to God and was given the Ten Commandments; but he never got to the Promised Land, due to disobedience of God's instructions. Moses lived through all that; but it was 3,500 years later when in his glorified body, he was awarded the great privilege to enter the Promised Land with Elijah on the Mount of Transfiguration to be with Christ in His hour of need (Matt. 17:3). This scenario should encourage us all to obey God's plan for our lives and continue to move forward with our dreams and visions, even when we don't feel adequate to the calling. God so often uses ordinary people to do extraordinary accomplishments. Is He calling you?

It was 1997. I had a call to write a book. Yet, like so many of you, I had several time dilemmas: a full-time corporate job with an average of fifty-six hours per week; CEO of my own company (which requires international travel); husband to a beautiful wife; father of two energetic boys; and a committed passion for full-time Christian ministry. As He did to Moses,

God gave me a call and direction to start writing this book. But my excuse was the lack of any more time in the day to commit to this project, and I felt discouraged because I kept hearing a voice in my head saying, "You'll never finish the book." Yet, I still had a strong tugging from the Holy Spirit to move forward with this project. But how? The solution was to set aside small chunks of time. So I started writing each chapter individually and called them "chapter books" or "mini-series books."

Now here I am many years later to testify that the book is finished! Needless to say, the majority of my research and much of my writing was done either over the Atlantic or Pacific oceans or in airports or hotels in France, Germany, Holland, Hong Kong, China, Japan, South Korea, India, etc.

Look Up For Your Redemption Is Near is a compiled overview of what the Bible has to say about the past, present and future events of history. A brief synopsis starts with biblical history and then builds a solid foundation on the things, events, and people which God foretells. At this time in history, many prophecies have already come to pass just as foretold.

Next, I move into archeology and the Bible. This section lays down some facts and archeological discoveries that support the Bible. I move on to a current issue today—Babylon and its importance in prophecy in history and the future. This leads into end times—Israel's place in prophecy, the rapture of the Church, the coming prominent world leaders, apocalyptic judgments the world will face, and the Second Coming of Christ.

As a side note, I am not a fan of religion, because religion is man's attempt to reach God. Faith is based on the teachings, promises and truths of God's Word, often spoken to us via Christ our Lord or the Holy Spirit. Keep in mind that throughout all biblical writings, there are ample verses about God's promises and prophecies, especially in the books of Daniel and Revelation, that have already been fulfilled or are being fulfilled as this book is being written. There are still several major events, prophecies, and destinies to be completed before Redemption. In particular, these two books will be the primary focus of this study and will help you, the reader, to better understand two of the most prophetic books in all of history, including the Old and New Testaments.

My prayer is that from this study, your eyes will be opened to what Scripture has to say regarding the Second Coming of our Lord and Savior, Jesus Christ. My passion has been to present the Scriptures in an accurate and easy-to-understand way so you can see, comprehend and accept what God (Father, Son, and Holy Spirit) is trying to communicate to you with compassion and loving-kindness. Your part is to do as the Bereans did in Acts 17:11 and search out the Scriptures diligently to discern what the Holy Spirit is telling and calling you to do.

May the peace and guidance of the Holy Spirit be with you and your studies of the Scriptures.

In the name above all names—Jesus Christ—I welcome you to this open door toward understanding your future.

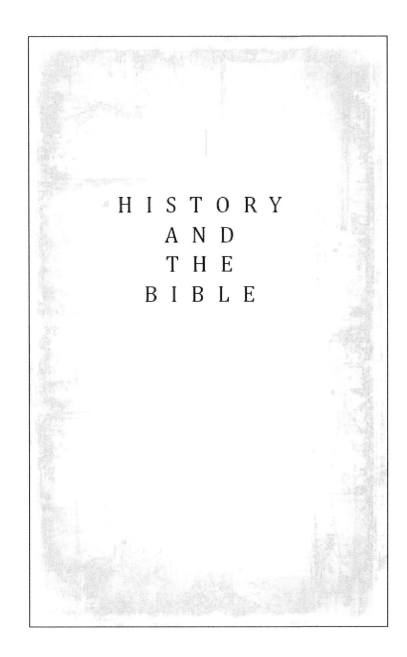

HISTORY
AND
THE
BIBLE

Chapter 1:
History and the Bible

Recently we entered a new millennium; it is obvious that mankind in his emptiness is reaching out and searching for the truth. Through the New Age movement, humans have turned to meditation, Eastern philosophy, and other ways to become self-reliant. Since mankind is searching for the truth, I felt it appropriate to start this series by sharing some of God's prophecies and their fulfillment as recorded in history. I encourage you to go to the library and read up on the early leaders in world history, as well as the nation of Israel. You will learn some very fascinating facts and you may have your eyes and heart opened; then you will look up and recognize that your redemption is near.

History shows that the first world empire was that of Babylon (586 BC), under the reign of Nebuchadnezzar, who was then conquered by the Medes and Persians under the command of Cyrus. Next came the Grecian Empire under the command of Alexander the Great. Finally, the last world empire was Rome, headed by Julius Caesar, among others.

Rome, in the first century, conquered the civilized world. Since the Roman Empire, we have not had a world empire, although many leaders have tried (for example, Napoleon and Hitler). Leaders have come and gone and will do so until the end of this life as we know it. But, the leadership of God has and will continue throughout history. He has provided windows to His plans by putting prophecies into His "map book"—The Holy Bible.

One such incident is recorded in Daniel 2 when King Nebuchadnezzar (King of Babylon) had a dream. "The king said to them: 'I had a dream and my spirit is anxious to understand the dream'" (Dan. 2:3 NASB). Not knowing what it meant, he called in his magicians, conjurers, sorcerers, and master astrologers to interpret its meaning. They asked the king to tell them the dream and then they would take time to learn and declare the interpretation. But the king said,

"The command from me is firm: if you do not make known to me the dream and its interpretation, you will be torn limb from limb and your houses will be made a rubbish heap. But if you declare the dream and its interpretation, you will receive from me gifts and a reward and great honor; therefore declare to me the dream and its interpretation" (Dan. 2:5b-6 NASB).

In Nebuchadnezzar's dream (Dan. 2:31–35), he saw a large statue with a head of gold, chest, and arms of silver, belly and thighs of bronze, legs of iron, and feet made partly of iron and partly of clay. He saw a rock being carved out, but not by human hands. The rock smashed the statue on its feet, destroying it without leaving a trace, and then the rock that destroyed the statue became an awesome mountain and filled the earth.

None of the wise men were able. So the king sent out a decree to kill all the wise men; this included Daniel (who was a prophet of God) and his friends. But Daniel used discretion and discernment and spoke to the captain of the king's bodyguards, Arioch, regarding the reason for the decree. He was permitted to go to the king, and he requested time to learn about the dream and the interpretation.

Daniel answered in the presence of the king, and said, "The secret which the king hath demanded cannot the wise men, the astrologers, the magicians, the soothsayers, shew unto the king. But there is a God in heaven that revealeth secrets, and maketh known to the king Nebuchadnezzar what shall be in the latter days." (Dan. 2:27–28).

God did reveal the dream to Daniel, as the interpretation. The interpretation (Daniel 2:36–45) was that the head of gold represented King Nebuchadnezzar and his kingdom, Babylon. The chest and arms represented two kingdoms combining their strength, and we now know that these two kingdoms were the Medes and the Persians. Daniel continued with the interpretation, telling the king that a third kingdom would rule the earth, as represented by the belly and thighs of bronze. This was the Grecian Empire. Finally, a fourth kingdom, strong as iron, would rule and crush all. Clearly, this describes the Roman Empire, whose brute force dominated the world. The Roman Empire would later collapse from within and become the individual countries of Europe. This fulfilled the next prophecy, which Daniel explained as a kingdom that would divide into smaller and weaker nations as iron and clay. He then added:

And in the days of these kings shall the God of heaven set up a kingdom, which shall never be destroyed: and the kingdom shall not be left to other people, but it shall break in pieces and consume all these kingdoms, and it shall stand forever (Dan. 2:44).

So as can be seen now, the Bible's coming events.

This then leads to another astonishing prophecy found in the book of Isaiah. It describes how Cyrus will conquer Babylon. "This is what the LORD says to his anointed, to Cyrus, whose right hand I take hold of to subdue nations before him and to strip kings of their armor, to open doors before him so that gates will not be shut (Isa. 45:1 NIV).

This prophecy was written 150 years before the event took place, and it describes how Cyrus would enter the city. History records that at that time, Babylon was a city with walls so high and wide it would be almost impossible to conquer. Yet Cyrus (of the Medes and Persians) did conquer Babylon by backing up the Euphrates River and going under the walls. There he found the gates of the city left open. Then he overtook the city by complete surprise.

When Cyrus came into power, Daniel showed him that his name was written in the scrolls of Isaiah's writings. Cyrus was so awestruck by this that it influenced his decision to allow the Jews to leave Babylon and return to Jerusalem.

Continuing with Bible prophecies, Psalm 22 contains a prophecy that predicts the crucifixion of Christ thousands of years before the crucifixion was even thought of. "They pierced my hands and my feet" (Psalm 22:16).

Another prophecy is found in the book of Matthew as Jesus was leaving the temple: "And Jesus said unto them, See ye, not all these things? Verily I say unto you, there shall not be left here one stone upon another that shall not be thrown down" (Matt. 24:2).

History records that when Titus took the city of Jerusalem in 70 AD, a soldier set fire to the temple, and all the gold melted into the cracks of the rocks. The soldiers then disassembled the temple stone by stone, gathering up all the gold—fulfilling yet another prophecy.

Before I was a believer in Christ, I was quite skeptical about the Bible and passages like these. My question was, how do I know that the Bible was not written after the fact? I mean, it would not seem like a difficult task to "predict" something that has already happened. As this question kept entering my mind, I felt a need to do some research into history. My research led me to the amazing Dead Sea Scrolls, which were discovered in 1947. These consist of nearly 500 scrolls and fragments, including the complete book of Isaiah.

Archaeologists have been able to date these scrolls to over 2,500 years ago.

This led to my researching the history of the nation of Israel, both ancient and modern day. I found that in the 1800s all the land in the region was neglected by the Arabs and Turks. They cut down all the trees, creating a marshland. In the 1930s, during the Zionist movement, the Jews gradually purchased back the land and started planting trees. Today, Israel is the fourth largest producer of fruit in the world. Israel fruit for all of Europe during the winter. In Ezekiel 36, the Lord states:

"'They will say, "This land that was laid waste has become like the garden of Eden; the cities that were lying in ruins, desolate and destroyed, are now fortified and inhabited." Then the nations around you that remain will know that I the LORD have rebuilt what was destroyed and have replanted what was desolate. I the LORD have spoken, and I will do it'" (Ezek. 36:35–36 NIV).

Could this passage be a coincidence? Or was God telling His people He had decreed it and, yes, it would happen? Did you know that Israel is the only country in the world that has lost its land yet never lost its citizenship? The Jews were dispersed around the world; and yet on May 14, 1948, Israel became a nation, thus fulfilling the prophecy of Ezekiel 37:21: "This is what the Sovereign LORD says: I will take the Israelites out of the nations where they have gone. I will gather them from all around and bring them back into their land" (NIV). Again I would ask the question: Is this a coincidence? Or did the Lord forewarn His people of events that would take place?

In 1967, during the Six-Day War, Israel again defended its land; and yet again, God's Word was fulfilled: "I will bless those who bless you, and whoever curses you I will curse" (Gen. 12:3 NIV). In October of 1973, during Yom Kippur, Syria and Egypt attacked Israel from opposite ends. Since Yom Kippur is the Jews' holiest day of the year, the Israelis were not militarily prepared for battle. The Syrians attacked a twenty-mile area with nearly 1,200 tanks, while Egypt had 3,000 tanks and heavy artillery. With minimal support, the Israeli army managed to again overthrow their attackers. Incidentally, Jerusalem has had more wars fought at its gates than any other city in the world.

We are living in very exciting times, and we are seeing the fulfillment of the Lord's words come to pass. In the early 1900s, a British scholar condemned the Bible as a hoax because of a verse stating that every people, tribe, language, and nation will witness an event that takes place (Rev. 11:9). This was impossible before TV was invented. Yes, biblical prophecy is unfolding in front of our eyes daily thanks to this invention and that of the computer and the Internet. Recently on a return flight from Europe, a young student from Switzerland was sitting next to me. He saw me reading my Bible and told me that his grandmother had been saying for years that Christ is coming back, which to him seemed like a myth. I quickly pointed out Luke 21, which says that knowledge will be increased in the end times and when we see and hear of these events taking place we are to look up because our redemption is drawing near.

The book of Revelation states, "What must soon take place" (Rev. 1:1 NIV). In the original Greek language, the word soon means "rapidly" (similar to a domino effect). This indicates that once it is ready to happen, it will happen quickly. Then I showed him Revelation 13:17, which talks about a cashless society: "No one could buy or sell unless he had the mark, which is the name of the beast or the number of his name" (NIV). If you had considered the idea of a cashless society twenty-five years ago, you would have said, "No way...not possible!"

However, today, with ATMs, point of sale, electronic banking, etc., one can no longer say there is no way it will not come to pass. Think about it: we are almost totally a cashless society at the time of this writing. The concept of a cashless society might seem very attractive—especially to the IRS. The consumer might also find it extremely convenient to not worry about cash on hand.

When governments finally do go cashless, think of advantages: the crime rate would probably decrease greatly; banks and merchants would not have to worry about checks bouncing; and drug lords would be left with large amounts of cash they would not be able to account for.

When I'm traveling abroad, it is easiest to use ATMs to receive each country's currency; that way I do not have to pay a bank commission fee and I get the current international market exchange rate.

Revelation 13:17 then goes on to foretell the new world leader who will give everyone a mark on their right hand or forehead: "the mark, which is the name of the beast or the number of his name" (NIV). Could this mark be a computer chip or possibly a laser tattoo? Today in the US, animals can be tagged by injecting a microchip in them. In Singapore, during the spring of 1998, a microchip was installed on a man's forehead. That same spring, an article in Time Magazine reported on the benefits of a cashless society.

Just imagine going to buy groceries and having the cashier scan your forehead to deduct your payment. It is also interesting to note that the FDA will not approve a drug, medicine, or technology until it has been tested for seven years. If this type of technology is under development now (perhaps in a testing period), could we be within seven years of a cashless society? Today, as we watch the news and read the paper, we find many current events are in line with Bible prophecy.

Let's return to Daniel and the dream interpretation that was discussed regarding the world empires that have already reigned. What about the rest of the prophecy referring to the feet of the statue made of iron and clay? And what about the rock that is cut from a mountain, not by human hands, and later crushes the feet and toes of the statue (Dan. 2:41–45)?

Let's examine the prophecy by looking at the feet and toes of the statue that emerge from the legs of iron, which history has defined as being the Roman Empire. This prophecy implies that the fourth empire (Rome) will reunite, with ten nations, both stronger and weaker, forming a united community. This is fascinating because even before the 1990s when the Berlin Wall came down, the European countries were starting to form a trade association, which has come to be known as the European Union (EU).

In the past, when traveling through Europe, you would have to stop at border patrols in each country and receive a passport entry. Today, your first port of entry into Europe is the only passport stamp needed. This makes it easier to travel around Europe. Also, as of January 1, 1999, the euro was adopted, giving Europe only one currency (excluding the UK, Sweden, and Switzerland).

Looking back fifty years at Nazi Germany and how Hitler attacked and destroyed most of Europe, could anyone have predicted then that these countries would someday unite, and give up their military and currency? Doubtful! Hundreds of years earlier, the Bible predicted it, and we are now seeing and experiencing this with our own eyes.

The Lord spoke it then, and it is happening now. We must also note that the Lord said He has given His Word to "show his servants what must soon take place" (Rev. 1:1 NIV). In other words, the word coincidence is not in the Lord's vocabulary!

In the New Testament, the Pharisees asked Jesus to perform a miracle and Jesus answered them:

> "A wicked and adulterous generation asks for a miraculous sign! But none will be given it except the sign of the prophet Jonah. For as Jonah was three days and three nights in the belly of a huge fish, so the Son of Man will be three days and three nights in the heart of the earth" (Matt. 12:39–40 NIV).

The Bible has laid out history, which included the past, present, and most importantly, the future. Jesus also stated, "I have come in my Father's name, and you do not accept me; but if someone else comes in his name, you will accept him" (John 5:43 NIV).

Could this perhaps be the new charismatic world leader? Daniel's prophecy declares that the next world leader will come out of the Roman Empire (or be of Roman descent) and will establish a one-world government. This world leader is known as the Antichrist. The word anti in Greek means "instead of" or "other than." We also read in Revelation 6:2 of this leader appears on the scene. He is identified as a rider of a white horse.

Daniel 9 refers to seventy-seven-year periods declared upon the nation of Israel. Sixty-nine of the seventy-seven-year periods has been fulfilled by Christ's appearing, suffering, and dying for our sins, which opened the door to everlasting life for all who accept Jesus Christ as their Lord and Savior. The last seven-year cycle has not started yet, and it will be ushered in by the world leader. Daniel refers to him, saying he will make a treaty with the nation of Israel and rebuild their temple, and it will be completed.

After ruling for three and a half years, the Antichrist will walk into the temple and enter into the Holy of Holies and claim he is the Christ, which, in biblical terms, is the "abomination of desolation."

So, according to the book of Daniel, this leader will come from the Roman Empire and bring peace to Israel. If you ask a Jewish scholar who their Messiah will be (for Jews do not believe that Christ is the Messiah), they will tell you that the Messiah will bring peace to Israel and rebuild the temple. The Bible describes this new leader as a charismatic man who brings peace to the earth and seems to solve economic problems. The world will follow him, love him and support and participate in his forming of a one-world government.

Think about this scenario. In the last fifty years, we have seen NATO emerge as a world peacekeeper (to some degree); the Soviet Union collapse; and the United States of America closing many military bases, thus decreasing military manpower. Could this all be part of God's plan to allow a one-world government? This may be hard to visualize. Yet, after World War II, who would have thought that all the nations of Europe would be joining forces with Germany, as we have seen happen?

More and more of the various countries' governments are intertwining with their neighbors, and more and more of the Bible's prophecies are coming true. Every day new, major changes take place. Some people know about it, and the majority of others are hidden and are slowly infiltrating the general population. Civilizations are struggling just to keep up with all these new changes.

Could the rule of the Antichrist be sooner than we think? Are we ready for a one-world government? Are we ready for his flattering charisma, his extensive knowledge and skill in languages, his ability to perform what looks miraculous, his powerful political aura, and his massive ego that will overpower and blind the masses to all the selfish, lawless, and wonder-working evils of his reign? It is predicted that he will become a formidable power like none other.

Revelation 13:3 talks about the world leader surviving an assassination attempt later into his reign and then miraculously recovering from a fatal wound. The people of the earth are so astonished that they pledge their worship to him.

Revelation 13:11–13 refers to the leader's trusted associate, believed to be a religious figure, performing miracles and wonders also. In referring to the end times, Daniel 12:11 states that after the world leader abolishes the regular sacrifices and desecrates the Holy of Holies (with the "abomination of desolation"), there will be 1,290 days until the end of life as we know it.

After this event, the wrath of God will be poured out upon the earth (as described in Revelation 6-19). The final battle, the Battle of Armageddon (Rev. 16:16), will take place in the valley of Megiddo. And from here, we go back to the conclusion of Daniel's prophecy:

> The God of heaven will set up a kingdom that will never be destroyed...It will crush all those kingdoms and bring them to an end, but it will endure forever. This refers back to the vision of the rock cut out of a mountain, but not by human hands (Dan. 2:44–45 NIV).

Revelation 19:11 says, "And I saw heaven opened, and behold a white horse, and sat upon him was called Faithful and True, and in righteousness he dot, judge and make war."

The Bible teaches that man is made for eternal life. Although our flesh only lives for so long, our spirits and souls shall live for eternity in either heaven or hell. It is so hard to be in this world and not of this world: "For he that soweth to his flesh shall of the flesh reap corruption; but he that soweth to the Spirit shall of the Spirit reap life everlasting" (Gal. 6:8).

As children of God, we have the Holy Spirit dwelling inside us, and we can understand spiritual things. Remember, the flesh seeks this world's realities and does not understand the power of our Lord.

Chapter 2:
Archaeology's Impact on the Bible

Within the last 150 years, a great phenomenon has developed in the field of archeology. Thanks to the many archeologists and the numerous hours that have been spent searching for the truth about the history of various civilizations, exciting new facts have been revealed. These researchers have furnished background materials that illustrate, illuminate and authenticate the stories, lives, geography, and topography in the Old and New Testaments. Because of today's growing interest in the signs of the times and the daily reports on what is happening in our world and how it is fitting into biblical prophecy, there is great enthusiasm for archeology and the proof it brings to the Scriptures. The Lord said, "Blessed are those who have not seen and yet have believed" (John 20:29). Each of us lives by faith every day, yet a non-believer still wants more evidence to believe something that this man called Jesus said more than 2,000 years ago. A Christian has believed and received the knowledge and assurance of the Holy Spirit's indwelling in his heart by faith (Romans 8:16). The changes taking place in his own life are strong evidence of His true power.

The Bible is the most unique collection of books in all of history. It is truly amazing, and there is evidence continually being discovered. The proof is often found in archives and museums around the world. Or, it may be discovered under the "sands of time."

In the summer of 2007, the Natural Museum of History in San Diego, California, displayed the Dead Sea Scrolls, ancient texts discovered initially by Bedouin goatherds. From 1947 through 1956, archeologists explored eleven caves near Khirbet, Qumran, which is northeast of the Dead Sea in Israel. These scrolls date from 250 BC to AD 68. So far, there are 207 biblical manuscripts, confirming the contents of most of the books of the Old Testament. Yes, these transcripts have been verified as being written thousands of years ago.

My family and I had the privilege of being eyewitnesses to the scrolls, codices, and Roman coins, along with other artifacts, all well preserved. These ancient codices (Scriptures) were written between AD 900 and AD 1100. Imagine seeing these documented artifacts that verify that the Bible was written thousands of years ago! This should make all of us stop and think about the truths God ordained and placed into this magnificent one-of-a-kind book. Every person who reads and accepts these premises can benefit eternally. What was the truth then is also true now and will be in the future, for all these truths are eternal. All predicted prophecies will be completed at the time of the Second Coming of Christ.

We already know that the Bible has predicted many historical events and truths that have come to pass and have been documented. Although the Bible is the most-read book in the history of the world, some still choose to refuse to believe in these writings and God, who inspired them.

In regards to the New Testament writings, 24,633 manuscripts have been discovered and preserved. Some of these manuscripts, such as the Gospel of Mark written as an eyewitness account of Jesus, date back to AD 68. The entire New Testament (minus eleven verses) has been reconstructed from the Early Church Fathers' writings and sermons. This consists of 86,489 quotes. What a bold testament and legacy! Our Lord and Savior have preserved His Word throughout these thousands of years. The conclusion can be drawn then that what we read today is the same text that was written and read by the early Fathers, the called leaders, kings, prophets, priests, disciples, and apostles.

As stated earlier, museums around the world display ancient artifacts that support the timeline of events in the Bible, including the names of world leaders (pharaohs, kings, rulers, etc.). In Israel, it is possible to go to the synagogues in Capernaum (where Jesus would often preach) and on to Caesarea, Jerusalem, Bethlehem, Nazareth, and other geographical areas where Jesus walked, taught, and lived. Outside of Israel, visit Rome (e.g., the coliseum and the forum), Turkey (Ephesus), Syria (Damascus), Egypt, Greece (Corinth), and other historical areas, buildings, graves, hills, and cities where many archeological sites and structures have been discovered and documented. All these authenticate the history, timeline, and persons involved during that period of history. Yes, even evidence of the "Big Flood" shows up in geological digs around the world. Every culture has a story passed down about the Big Flood. Archeologists have found fossils of fish and other sea creatures in mountain ranges around the world, even the Himalayas.

Psalm 19:1 says, "The heavens declare the glory of God, and the firmament showeth his handiwork." Science has continued to unravel the secrets of the universe, and these scientists continue to find that what the Bible said so many years ago is all true and accurate. New scientific evidence is daily proving the truth of a Creator. DNA, as an example, is too complex to have evolved via random evolution. The human body is perfect evidence of the carefulness of the creation plan. The complexity of the "Heavens" and many universes show absolute order and structure, a well-planned design of motion—perfect in every way. Take time to see the examples of a well-planned orderly design everywhere around us. There is no place on earth without the magnificent presence and touch of God, and today's archeology is providing more and more evidence of the Creator and the fulfillment of His prophecies in the Scriptures.

In this book, called the Bible are to be found the words of God; a history of the earth, civilizations, and time; and stories of how God uses ordinary people to do extraordinary tasks and how they become extraordinary leaders. He has given us a continuous road map to everlasting Life. The Bible is our "Basic Instructions Before Leaving Earth." If all this archeological evidence brings conviction to your heart, and you seek out God and follow His instructions, God will send the Holy Spirit to lead you towards "the way, the truth, and the life. No one may come to the Father except through God's only Begotten Son" (see John 14:6 and John 3:16).

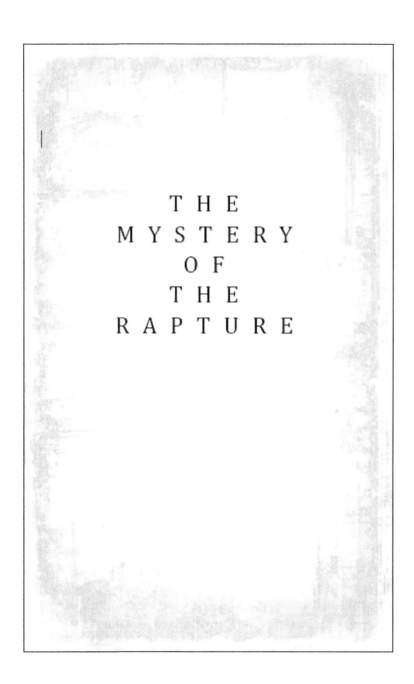

THE MYSTERY OF THE RAPTURE

Chapter 3:
The Mystery of the Rapture

So you say you're a good person, you believe in God, you live your life showing respect to others and you enjoy the pleasures of life, yet you wonder if this is all there is. As you watch TV, you notice current events, movies, and lifestyles that promote violence, sex, and pleasure. Music, movies, and commercials advertise the pleasures of man's flesh, which leads to the decay of our society due to media corruption. It makes you think, what is this world coming to?

As a minister and Bible teacher, I often get asked the same questions. Is the end near? Is the earth going to be wiped out? Why would a God of love do this to man? On the other hand, I get the questions answered by people saying, "I do not think God would destroy the earth, " I believe that good people will go to heaven, "or "I think there are many ways to heaven and being a good person is all that counts. After all, Jesus says if you believe in Him, you will be saved." These are all questions and answers that we will be addressing in this chapter.

When asked about the end, I first start with the past, something that has already taken place. I usually start with history and the Bible, showing past and current events that have taken place, details of which can be found in libraries, encyclopedias, newspapers, media, and, of course, the Bible. Once we have a sense that what God said would happen has happened, end times prophecies are more tangible and acceptable.

Let's start with a synopsis of the end times while reviewing some previously discussed doctrines. According to the Bible, the next prophesied event will be the Body of Christ (Christians) being removed from the earth. This is referred to as the Rapture of the Church.

After the Rapture, a world leader emerges for seven years, bringing peace to the earth. He will confirm a treaty between Israel and Palestine and issue orders for the rebuilding of the temple in Jerusalem. According to the book of Daniel, this world leader will be of European descent. The Bible explains that this world leader will be a charismatic man who brings about economic prosperity. The world will embrace him. He will set up a one-world government as well as a one-world religion (with the help of a trusted partner), and he will then usher in a cashless society. An assassination attempt will be made on his life, and he will lose his right eye and the use of his right arm (Zech. 11:17). His miraculous recovery will astound the world, and it will marvel over him to such a degree that many will worship him as "God."(Rev. 13:12–15). After three and a half years, he will walk into the temple in Jerusalem and demand to be worshiped (this is known as the "abomination of desolation").

At this time, the wrath of God will be poured out upon the earth for a final period of three and a half years (completing a total of seven years), bringing earthquakes, famines, pestilence, and wars. At the end of these seven years, the nations of the earth will gather for a battle, which will take place in the valley of Megiddo (also known as Armageddon) in Israel. Then the Lord Himself will come down with His Church (the Christians) and wipe out the armies of the world. After this, there will be what is known as the Millennium Reign of Christ, where Christ rules on the earth with His saints (believers) for 1,000 years. After a thousand years will come the final judgment.

"Wow!" you say, "pretty heavy!" To get a grasp of this, as mentioned earlier, you need to realize that everything that God has predicted has happened. Therefore, since our Lord's prophecies have been and continue to be 100 percent accurate, end-time prophecies will be 100 percent accurate as well.

Again, it is a reminder to look up and stop thinking only of the things of this world. Look! Take an intense look at creation, the universe, and beyond to understand what our creator, the Lord Jesus Christ, is capable of. The Bible states in Genesis 1:1–19 that the Lord spoke into existence the heavens and the earth. Isaiah 40:12 refers to God measuring the universe with the span of His hand: "Who hath measured the waters in the hollow of his hand, and meted out heaven with the span, and comprehended the dust of the earth in a measure, and weighed the mountains in scales, and the hills in a balance?" It is necessary to realize that we as humans can only comprehend a three-dimensional world, whereas God is outside the domain of time and can do things we are not yet capable of understanding. Psalm 19:1 states, "The heavens declare the glory of God." In other words, the sky, the sun, the moon, and the stars declare to us the awesome power of our Lord. It is also interesting to note that with modern-day technology (NASA, satellites, etc.) we seem to discover more and more about our universe, which just shows us how great our God is.

The Bible tells us that God knows everything from beginning to end (Rev. 22:13). To better understand this, let's use the analogy of a street parade. We, as viewers standing at a particular corner, can only witness the parade as it passes by, whereas God sees everything from start to finish, all at one time (like a newscaster or emcee would see the entire parade from a blimp or helicopter while providing commentary on the parade).

Let's get back to the Rapture of the Church. "The Rapture of the church," you say, "what is that? The word rapture is not even in my Bible. "Well, in a sense, you're right. The word rapture is not in the English Bible; however, you can find it in the Latin Vulgate as the word rapturous, from which we get our English word rapture. In the original Greek language, the word is harpoons, which means "snatched away" (or "taken by force"), which is also paraphrased as "caught up." We are not sure how this will happen—either we Christians will leave our bodies or our bodies will be taken away—but what we do know is that the Bible says we will be caught up (harpoons) in the clouds to meet the Lord. "Then we which are alive and remain shall be caught up together with them in the clouds, to meet the Lord in the air: and so shall we ever be with the Lord" (1 Thess. 4:17). In other words, there is a generation that will never die. Imagine, if our bodies are physically taken, the world will probably attribute the event to aliens or some kind of phenomenon.

First Corinthians 15:51–53 states,

> "Behold, I shew you a mystery; We shall not all sleep, but we shall all be changed; In a moment, in the twinkling of an eye, at the last trump: for the trumpet shall sound, and the dead shall be raised incorruptible, and we shall be changed. For this corruptible must put on in corruption, and this mortal must put on immortality."

Christ assures us that we will receive our new bodies and meet Him in the clouds because heaven is out of this world. This might be compared to an astronaut who is preparing to go into outer space. To accomplish this feat, a specially designed suit with multiple functions must be put on. So shall it be for all of us who are preparing for Christ's Second Coming. At the time of the Rapture, we too will immediately put on a new, specially designed suit (body) to make the journey.

So your next question is, "When will this happen?" The answer is that no man knows the hour or the day. "But of that day and hour no one knows, not even the angels of heaven, nor the Son, but the Father alone" (Matt. 24:36 NASB).

However, Jesus spoke of watching for signs of the end: "When these things begin to take place, stand up and lift your heads because your redemption is drawing near" (Luke 21:28 NIV).

Signs that the Bible has prophesied include:

❷ Israel becoming a nation (Ezek. 37)

❷ Israel became like the garden of Eden and produce fruit for the world (Ezek. 36)

❷ Europe joined forces and became a nation (Daniel 2)

Jesus also stated, "Just as it was in the days of Noah, so also will it be in the days of the Son of Man" (Luke 17:26 NIV). In the days of Noah, man was corrupt, filled with evil, and had no fear of God. Noah preached repentance for 120 years as he built his ark. People looked at Noah as if he were crazy, for in those days it had never rained—the earth was surrounded with a canopy of light mist (Gen. 2:6). Can you imagine how crazy it would be to see a man building a huge ship, saying that a flood was coming? No one believed Noah, yet the flood did come (archaeologists have acknowledged findings consistent with a worldwide flood).

Revelation 4:1 starts with the word metatosa, which is a Greek word meaning "after these things." We would then ask, "After what things?" Before this word metatosa Revelation chapters 2 and 3 talk about "the seven churches." The seven churches represent church history, speaking of the past as well as present-day churches. Therefore, in Revelation 4:1, after the Church is discussed, the writer is caught up (harpoons). We believe this refers to the Rapture of the Church. After this verse, the events of chapters 4 and 5 take place in heaven, where Christians are worshiping together as Christ's bride, preparing for the wedding supper feast.

It is interesting to note that when Christ comes back for His Church, He will meet us in the clouds (Acts 1:9–11; 1 Thess. 4:17) and then bring us into His Father's home for seven years. Later, when we return with Him, He will introduce His bride (the Church) to the world. This is similar to the Jewish traditions of marriage. After a Jewish boy confirmed his engagement with his bride-to-be, he went to his father's home to prepare a house for her. The custom was that the couple would live on his father's estate. The father would watch and inspect as the son built, and finally, upon the father's approval, the son would be sent to get his bride. In the meantime, the bride would have chosen her bridesmaids, who would watch the progress of the house. When they saw that it was almost finished, they let the bride know, and they watched for the coming of the groom. (Jesus gives a parable about this in Matthew 25, about the ten virgins.) As the groom came, the bride met him halfway. They then had a marriage ceremony and a honeymoon for seven days, and upon their return, they were introduced to their guests as husband and wife.

In John 14:2, Christ stated, "In my Father's house are many mansions: if it were not so, I would have told you. I go to prepare a place for you." When God is ready and has gathered His people (the fulfillment of the Gentiles, as described in Romans 11:25), then He will send His Son, Jesus Christ, to meet us (the Church) in the clouds (halfway, if you will) (Acts 1:9–11; 1 Thess. 4:17). From there, we will enjoy the Marriage Supper of the Lamb for seven years; upon our return, Christ will introduce His Bride to the world:

> Let us rejoice and be glad and give the glory to Him,
> for the marriage of the Lamb has come and His bride
> has made herself ready." It was given to her to clothe

herself in fine linen, bright and clean; for the fine linen
are the righteous acts of the saints (Rev. 19:7–8 NASB).

On Earth, during these seven years, there will be three and a half years of peace led by the new world leader. Then the wrath of God will be poured out upon Christ-rejecting earth for the remaining three and a half years. Because our God is loving, He will not require Christians to endure the great tribulation that will be poured out upon the earth, but He will save us via the Rapture. Revelation 3:10 states, "Since you have kept my command to endure patiently, I will also keep you from the hour of trial [or tribulation] that is going to come upon the whole world to test those who live on the earth" (NIV). Luke 21:36 states, "Watch ye therefore, and pray always, that ye may be accounted worthy to escape all these things that shall come to pass."

As a side note, events in the New Testament can also be found in the Old Testament. The Rapture is a good example. We all know of Noah and the flood. Now, if you recall, Noah was saved or protected from the flood by God. Noah was a representation of the 144,000 Jews that go through the tribulation yet are protected by Christ (Rev. 7:4). Noah's ancestor Enoch was a man who "walked with God; then he was no more because God took him away"(Gen. 5:24 NIV). Enoch was a representation of the Church, of the people who walk with Christ and who are Christ-like. Enoch was raptured, or caught up, just as the Church will be.

Another example of the Rapture can be found in Daniel 3. In this chapter, we read about King Nebuchadnezzar, who commanded all the people to bow down to his statue or they would be cast into a furnace. A11 the people bowed down except for three Hebrew young men: Shadrach, Meshach, and Abednego. They were cast into a furnace that was heated up seven times hotter than normal (representing the seven years of tribulation). Verse 25 tells us that one more man was walking in the furnace with them, one like the Son of God. The Hebrews are a representation of the 144,000 Jews that the Lord will protect during the tribulation (Rev. 7:4). An interesting question arises from this story: where was Daniel during the events? He is not mentioned here. We know that he was a godly man and he would not bow down to this image or any other, so, therefore, he was taken out of the situation (a representation of the Rapture).

Another Old Testament illustration of the Rapture can be found in Genesis 19 when Lot was spared from the destruction of Sodom and Gomorrah. The angel of the Lord took his hand and snatched him out of the city. Interestingly, the word for snatched in Hebrew is translated as "taken by force."

In the New Testament, in 2 Corinthians 12:2–4, we see Paul, who was caught up in the third heaven and had a view of paradise that was too awesome to describe. (Bible scholars believe that this incident occurred when Paul was stoned and left for dead, Acts 14:19.)

Another model of the Rapture occurs in Revelation 4:1 when John is told to "Come up hither" and he sees the throne of God.

So as you can see, the Rapture of the Church has been modeled throughout Scripture. Do you have a hard time believing that such an event will occur? When the disciples asked Jesus about the end times, Jesus said, "Therefore, you also be ready, for the Son of Man is coming at an hour you do not expect" (Matt. 24:44 NKJV). Additionally, we were told, "Two men will be in the field; one will be taken and the other left. Two women will be grinding with a hand mill; one will be taken and the other left" (Matt. 24:40–41 NIV). He then added, "But know this, that if the master of the house had known what hour the thief would come, he would have watched and not allowed his house to be broken into" (Matt. 24:43 NKJV). First

Thessalonians 5:1-4 says, "The day of the Lord will come like a thief in the night. While people are saying, 'Peace and safety,' destruction will come on them suddenly...But you, brothers, are not in darkness so that this day should surprise you" (NIV).

Throughout the New Testament, "the day of the Lord" is mentioned repeatedly. It is comforting to know that our Lord is long-suffering and does not wish for us to perish but that we should come to repentance (2 Peter 3:9). In other words, the Lord is waiting to gather in His Church. He is waiting for the "fulness of the Gentiles" (Romans 11:25), that they give their lives to Him. Then He will send His Son to gather us together. The Holy Spirit is convicting people of their sins, and Christians are spreading the gospel so that the world will know God's plan. In Revelation 1:1, where it refers to these things taking place quickly, the word quickly in Greek means "soon" or "suddenly." This means that, once the Lord is ready, it will happen like a domino effect (one event after another). The Bible was written so that we would not be ignorant of things to come. We need to live our lives in anticipation that our Lord and Savior will come at any time. Jesus says in Luke 19:13, "Occupy till I come." Christ wants us to daily go about His Father's business and be ready for His return.

Second Thessalonians 2 says that before the lawless one can come to power (referring to the Antichrist), the Church (the body of Christ) must be removed (Raptured). Once this happens, there will be looting and rioting in the streets. Just imagine hundreds of thousands of people from all over the world disappearing! This would cause world chaos, and cities would be in a panic. (Remember the Los Angeles riots or the Black Lives Matters movement) where cities around the country were uncontrollable?) This would be the perfect scenario in which a world leader could come to power and bring peace to the world.

Interestingly, Bible describes all of these events in such detail. As stated earlier, before I talk about the future I must first talk about the past and how God's prophecies have been fulfilled. Each day we see more and more of God's plans coming to pass. If I had told you in 1970 about a cashless society, you would have said I was crazy. No way would governments and people ever do away with cash as currency. Yet today, you can see how the world is moving in that direction, just as predicted in Revelation 13:16.

A friend of mine has an old Bible that was printed in 1820. Each time I see that Bible, it brings joy to my heart. That old Bible was printed almost two hundred years ago. Since then we have seen many of God's words come to pass. There is no other book in the world that has accurately predicted the future 100 percent of the time.

Until recently, it was hard to understand Ezekiel 38, which lists all of the countries that will oppose Israel. Prior toBeforeted States taking Saddam Hussein out of power, it seemed that Iraq would be the first to lead a war against Israel, yet the Bible omitted Iraq from the picture. It also amazes me that Iraq is modern-day Babylon, and the Bible states that Babylon will be a world economic center, the "Wall Street" of the Middle East!

You are not asked to understand the Rapture; you are just asked to believe it is a fact. Yes, it will happen according to Scripture. Our job as Christians (the word Christian means to be Christlike) is to tell people about our awesome Lord and Savior Jesus Christ and His plan for the future. Just imagine: you wake up one morning, turn on the news and hear that millions of people have vanished. Would you then believe it? Some people might believe; still, others will fall into this world's media corruption and believe this world's lie. When Christ walked the earth, many people who saw His miracles did not believe. Even the disciples themselves doubted our

Lord at times. Judas, being compelled by the power of Satan, denounced our Lord and chose the path to hell.

So the question is, what will you do with our Lord and Savior, Jesus Christ? Will you receive Him or reject Him? The Bible says that you are either for Him or against Him. In the Gospel of Matthew, Jesus said, "Therefore whoever confesses Me before men, him I will also confess before My Father who is in heaven. But whoever denies Me before men, him I will also deny before My Father who is in heaven"(Matt. 10:32–33 NKJV).

Revelation 3:20 says, "Behold, I stand at the door, and knock: if any man hears my voice, and open the door, I will come in. "Our Lord Jesus Christ is a gentleman—He will not force Himself into your life. Now the question is, Have you accepted the One and Only Son of God, Jesus Christ, into your heart, and are you planning to spend eternity with Him and all the raptured souls in heaven? Or are you planning to reject Him and spend eternity with Satan in hell? Your choice!

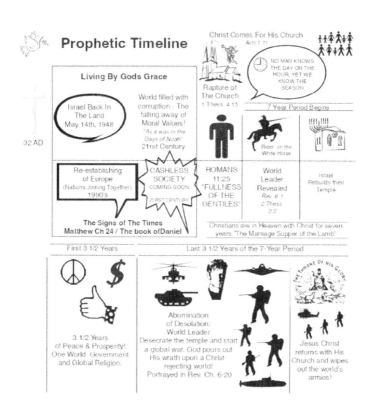

Chapter 4:
The Wrath of the Lamb

It's early Sunday morning. You put on a pot of tea, and as you open up the newspaper, the headline screams, "7.9 Earthquake in Argentina Kills 23,000!" Next, you read that a volcano has erupted in the Philippines, killing 18,000; a flood in the Midwest wiped out 7,000 people; and an earthquake in New York City has taken down the Statue of Liberty.

Wow, you say, what is going on? Every year it gets worse and worse. Is the world catastrophically changing? What's happening? As you go about your typical routine—work, golf, gym, parties and a little Sunday R and R—week after week, the same things occur, until one morning you open up the newspaper and read: "Millions of People Have Vanished from All over the World!" You quickly turn on the television. CNN, ABC, CBS, BBC—on every station, they are reporting on this phenomenon, yet the real issue is that the whole world is in an uproar. Complete chaos on Earth. Planes, automobiles, and trains have crashed; vehicles, houses, and stores have been abandoned, while gangs, criminals and the poor are looting and rioting in the streets. The United Nations enacts global military law as the military, police, and reserves gear up for battle. Hospitals are full; paramedics, firefighters, and emergency teams from all over the world are in a panic. There is so much disaster that the focus is on the chaos and not the phenomenon. For weeks this goes on and on, and finally, a charismatic leader emerges and reunites the world.

But you experience déjà vu. For you, remember a friend years ago telling you about an event in the Bible known as "the Rapture of the Church." You scroll through your Rolodex and call up your Christian friend, yet there is no answer. Is that just a coincidence?

According to the Bible, the next prophetic event is the removal of the Christians, and then there will be seven years left of world history. Revelation 4:1 is a passage that I believe shows the Rapture of the Church. After that, the fourth and fifth chapters of Revelation talk about a feast in heaven and a great multitude of people worshiping with praise. Revelation 6 introduces the rider on the white horse, the first of the five horsemen mentioned in Revelation. This is the Antichrist. The word "Antichrist" in Greek means "other than Christ" or "pseudo-Christ." (Note that this is not the same rider of the white horse that is found in Revelation 19, for that "rider" is our Lord and Savior Jesus Christ, whom I refer to as the fifth horseman.)

The Antichrist, or world leader, will, according to the book of Daniel, come to power and bring peace to the world. He will rebuild the temple in Jerusalem and be considered a wonderful and powerful man who seems to be the answer to the world's problems. This extremely charismatic man will be praised and accepted by the whole world.

It is amazing to me—and history teaches us—that man learns nothing from history. All the leaders in history that have come to power and gained control have done so under the same conditions—when nations were weak and in economic crisis. When Hitler came to power, he won the people over with his ideas and leadership. Yet later on, once he was in control, he showed his true self. The Bible prophesies that this world leader will come to power for seven years. During this time, he will set up a one-world government and a one-world religion and also bring about a cashless society.

If these scenarios seem far-fetched to you, then just review what it was like fifty years ago. If, in 1950, you were told Europe would join together and establish what is now known as the European Union (which is prophesied in Daniel as smaller and weaker nations joining together from within the Roman Empire), you would say it was impossible. No way would Holland, Belgium, France, and others join sides with Germany, especially after Hitler's brutal attack and destruction of these countries! Yet, it is so today. Now consider how each of these countries put aside the sovereignty of their currency and chose to enter into a one-currency system using the euro. If anyone had proposed such a suggestion to you back then, your response probably would have been that the person was a dreamer like Jules Verne in 20,000 Leagues Under the Sea.

And what about a cashless society, as prophesied in Revelation 13:17? Imagine living in 1860 or even 1960 and trying to grasp the concept of electronic banking, ATMs, point of sale, etc. Amazingly, today we have seen and experienced the convenience and benefits of a cashless society. The Bible teaches in Revelation 13:16–17 that the world leader will require everyone, both great and small, to have a mark on their right hand or forehead. Without the mark, no one will be able to buy or sell. These days, laser tattoos and microchip tagging of animals are realities. Sounds right in line with the Bible prophecy.

It is prophesied that a world leader will come to power, uniting the world and bringing peace to Israel by rebuilding the temple in Jerusalem. The Jews will praise him as the Messiah, which is interesting, given that in John 5:43, Jesus stated, "I have come in my Father's name, and you do not accept me; but if someone else comes in his name, you will accept him"(NIV). After the temple is rebuilt, according to Scripture (Dan. 12), the world leader will walk into the temple and demand to be worshiped, which is the "abomination of desolation." From that point on, the world leader will continue to show characteristics of his true nature, and Satan's hellish fury will explode upon the people and the earth. There will be no other power except the Beast (Antichrist's) and his cohorts, who will rule over all the earth. At this time, God will intervene and pour out His wrath upon a sinning people. The Wrath of the Lamb will come crashing down on all the earth—the great tribulation will begin.

The wrath of God, you say? What is that? Well, the Bible talks about the wrath of God in both the Old and New Testaments. It can be described as the Lord pouring out His anger and causing tribulation such as the world has never seen nor will they ever see again. In the Old Testament, this is referred to as "the time of Jacob's trouble" (Jeremiah 30:7), while in the New Testament, it is referred to as the great tribulation. There will be great earthquakes, famines, wars, and destruction.

In the book of Revelation, chapters 6–19, you'll find the prophecies about the plagues and destruction that will be poured out upon the earth. You'll read of the rider on the red horse having the authority to make war and remove peace from the earth. Also, to the rider on the red horse, authority is given to make peace and influence people to kill one another, as he will be given a great sword (Rev. 6:4 NKJV).

Next, you'll read a new theme about a black horse that causes inflation and famine—where a day's work will only buy a single meal. Then comes a pale horse, causing death by disease, hunger, and plagues:

> So I looked and behold, a pale horse. And the name of
> him who sat on it was Death, and Hades followed with

him. And power was given to them over a fourth of the earth, to kill with sword, with hunger, with death, and by the beasts of the earth (Rev. 6:8 NKJV).

Continuing, you will read about the seven trumpets that God gives to His seven angels to herald and release horrible destruction. The first angel will blow his horn, and hail and fire, mixed with blood, will be cast down on the earth. One-third of the earth will be set on fire, and one-third of all the grass and trees will be burnt. Try imagining this! Can you recall images of vast forest fires on TV, such as in Indonesia in recent years, and how the day became like night because of the smoke? What would it be like if one-third of the earth's forests were on fire? Would the earth be in darkness? This could be what Christ was talking about in Matthew 24:29, where He stated, in about tribulation, "The sun will be darkened, and the moon will not give its light" (NKJV).

Throughout the books of the Bible, we read of global catastrophes and disasters. In Zechariah 14:12, we read of end-time destruction that causes men's eyes to melt in their heads and their tongues to curl up and melt. Could this be a description of a nuclear attack?

Revelation describes the great battle of Armageddon, which is to take place in the valley of Megiddo. In this battle of all battles, the kings of the east will march with their army of 200 million soldiers (Rev. 9:16). Take note of this incredible prophecy to be fulfilled. When John wrote the book of Revelation, there weren't even 200 million people living on the earth! Yet today, we know China has an army of 200 million soldiers ready and available. Could it be China that is being described as the "king of the East?"

In Matthew 24, the disciples asked Jesus about the end times. Jesus told them,

"Take heed that no one deceives you. For many will come in My name, saying, 'I am the Christ,' and will deceive many. And you will hear of wars and rumors of wars. See that you are not troubled; for all these things must come to pass, but the end is not yet. For nation will rise against nation and kingdom against kingdom. And there will be famines, pestilences, and earthquakes in various places. All these are the beginning of sorrows...When you see the 'abomination of desolation,' spoken of by Daniel the prophet...then there will be great tribulation, such as has not been since the beginning of the world. And unless those days were shortened, no flesh would be saved...Then the sign of the Son of Man will appear in heaven, and then all the tribes of the earth will mourn, and they will see the Son of Man coming on the clouds of heaven with power and great glory"(Matt. 24:4–30 NKJV).

Yes! Christ will be coming back with His Church, the Christians. He is saying that the tribulation is going to be so bad that He will have to come back and defeat the enemy.

Interestingly, Matthew 24 parallels Revelations 6 and 19. In Revelation 6, the rider on the white horse comes and brings peace. That sounds like what Jesus refers to as the men who will deceive many and claim to be Christ (Matt. 24:4–5). Then there is the rider of the red horse, who is granted the power to take peace from the earth. As Jesus states in Matthew 24:6, there will be wars and rumors of wars. Then we read about the riders of the black and pale horses who bring famine and pestilence. And ultimately, we have Revelation 19:11, talking about the fifth horseman—our Lord and Savior—coming in the clouds with His saints, just like Jesus alludes to in Matthew 24:30. So we can see that Jesus gave His disciples a briefing at the end times.

The wrath of the Lamb can be described as the worst thing this earth will ever experience. The Bible even talks about demonic powers and demons being released upon the earth, as well as Satan worship.

Think about this: fifty years ago, people would never have imagined people would openly worship Satan, as we're seeing today in music, cults, and Satanic rituals. In the United States and around the world in the last decade, youths—elementary school age, high school age, and college age—have become mass murderers, going to public functions and schools with the intent to kill many. We even have youths killing their parents, friends, and family members!

The United States was established on biblical principles, and the Constitution was based on the Ten Commandments. Abraham Lincoln, one of the United States forefathers, said, "I believe the Bible is the best gift God has ever given to man. All the good from the Savior of the world is communicated to us in this book." And George Washington said, "It is impossible to rightly govern the world without God and the Bible." Our forefathers prayed and asked God for guidance, whereas today the Ten Commandments are being taken out of schools, courts, and public areas. Man has set his earthly laws—the results of which can be viewed each night on the evening news or in the local newspaper.

During the time of Noah, the world was so corrupt that God recognized His need to destroy the earth with a global flood. (It is interesting that modern scientists can prove there was a global flood. They estimate it to have occurred about 5,000 years ago and believe it was caused by a polar axis shift.) God spared Noah and his family. Then He made a covenant with Noah, stating, "All flesh shall never again be cut off by the water of the flood, neither shall there again be a flood to destroy the earth" (Gen. 9:11 NASB). He then gave Noah a rainbow as a confirmation of His covenant. In Matthew 24:37

Christ said, "As the days of Noah were, so shall also the coming of the Son of man be." God always gives us a warning of His actions. Because He is a loving God, He is "not willing that any should perish but that all should come to repentance"(2 Pet. 3:9 NKJV). In Noah's day, God showed His patience by giving the world 120 years to repent. Yet only Noah and his family believed in God and were saved. Could this be why God gave the apostle John the visions to write in the book of Revelation, so we are forewarned of what He has planned for our sinful world?

The doctrine of Christianity is based on Christ dying for our sins and three days later rising from the dead. Christ washed us clean with His blood and gave us a chance to live eternally in the presence of our Lord. We have the promise of salvation through the shedding of His blood.

All over the world, through all denominations of Christianity, people are praying for the return of Jesus Christ and for His Kingdom to come. In many churches today, sermons are being preached on end times and Christ's return. Yet, how many of us believe that Christ may come at any time? The Bible teaches that we are to anticipate His return at any minute and be ready. The Second Coming of Christ is preached more than any other event in the Bible. Jesus alludes to His coming over and over again throughout the New Testament. In Matthew 24:42, He said, "Watch therefore, for you do not know what hour your Lord is coming" (NKJV). And in Revelation 22:7, Jesus tells us, "Behold, I am coming quickly! Blessed is he who keeps the words of the prophecy of this book" (NKJV). Our selfish world is so busy worrying about "What's in it for me?" that they lose sight of why we are here on this earth—to worship the true and living God who created us. True believers in Christ are storing up their treasures in heaven and are patiently awaiting their rewards.

It is amazing to me that Jesus Christ is the most talked about man who ever walked the face of this earth. His presence is so strong that our yearly calendar is based on this remarkable man, along with the most celebrated event in the world—Christmas. Also, statistics show that the Bible is the most widely read book in all of history. With Jesus Christ's words having such an impact on the world, how many of us believe and follow them? It's hard to understand why anyone would choose to go through the great tribulation, which is a biblical promise to the non-believing world. The wrath of the Lamb will happen just as described in Revelation 6 to 19.

Yes, it is hard to understand that Christ will return as promised, and yes, it is hard to comprehend that His Word has been 100 percent accurate thus far. The Bible does foretell the future, and in the last fifty years, we have witnessed many Bible prophecies coming true, not to mention the progress being made on prophecies to be fulfilled in the future. For instance, on December 15, 1999, a press release was issued to NASDAQ, introducing a new e-commerce technology company whose aim is to implant a microchip in humans. This miniature digital transceiver will be able to act as a tracking device for e-business and for storing records.

You can bank on this technology as a winner. Revelation 13:16–17 foretells this and states that to live or purchase, you must accept this format that was predicted many hundreds of years ago. "And he causeth all, both small and great, rich and poor, free and bond, to receive a mark in their right hand, or their foreheads: And that no man might buy or sell, save he that had the mark."

With modern-day technology, we can now understand what the Bible is referring to. Just think, when believers 400 years ago read the book of Revelation, what faith they must have had to trust in Christ's predictions! It is amazing to think that 400 years ago, the method of transportation was horse and buggy. There was no way that someone could imagine airplanes, rockets, and space shuttles, the concept of wiping out the world with a single bomb or chemicals that can kill millions of people without their being aware of the danger. But that's what the Bible predicted! Can you imagine sitting in on a Bible study on the book of Revelation back in 1695? These passages would have seemed fictional and unimaginable. No wonder the general population thought Christians were crazy to even believe such utter nonsense! Well, today we can see this is not utter nonsense at all but the reality we are living daily.

In Daniel 12:4, Daniel was told to seal up the book until the end, when knowledge and understanding would increase. Could it now be the time when the end is near and knowledge has finally increased to catch up with the Bible's prophecies? And could now be the time when the future is now the present? The Bible has described the last seven-year period with so much detail and such precision that we must wake up and realize that we are getting closer to the return of our Lord and Savior, Jesus Christ.

The Bible has been given to us so that we will not be ignorant of things to come. Our Lord does not wish for any of us to perish, but for all to come to repentance and accept His grace and forgiveness (2 Pet. 3:9). We are washed clean by His blood, and all you have to do is ask Him to come into your heart, admit you are a sinner, repent of your sins, and turn and walk in His Spirit.

If you have not yet done so, you can ask Christ to come into your life right now, and He will forgive you of your sins and give you the promise of everlasting life.

T H E
S I G N S
O F
T H E
T I M E S

Chapter 5:
The Signs of the Times

It was mid-morning, on or about the eighth of Nisan, in the year AD 32. Jesus and His disciples were leaving the great temple in Jerusalem and heading towards the Mount of Olives. As they passed the temple, the disciples marveled at its beauty and magnificence. The temple was one of the greatest structures of that day, rising eight to ten stories high and sculptured in marble and gold. It was King Herod's mark on society and one of the wonders of the world. As the disciples turned to Jesus in awe, Christ simply stated: "Verily I say unto you, there shall not be left here one stone upon another, that shall not be thrown down" (Matt. 24:2). The disciples looked at each other in confusion and proceeded on their way up to the Mount of Olives.

Now, as they reached the Mount of Olives, four disciples, confused and wondering about what Christ had stated, came to Jesus privately and asked Christ three questions.

1.   *When will these things happen?*
2.   *What will be the sign of Your coming?*
3.   *When will be the end of the age?*

Before we get started in this overview of Matthew 24, which is known as the Olivet Discourse, you need to be aware that this is Christ's overview of end-time prophecy. Yes, Jesus Christ the Savior, the Healer, the Comforter and the Prophet will now, in His own words, give us a briefing on the end times.

> *"He who has an ear, let him hear" (Revelation 3:22 NKJV). And Jesus went out, and departed from the temple: and his disciples came to him for to shew him the buildings of the temple (Matt. 24:1). In this passage, Jesus left the temple for the last time. A few days earlier, He made His triumphal entry into Jerusalem riding on a donkey, fulfilling the prophecy of*

Zechariah 9:9 (NASB):

> *Rejoice greatly, O daughter of Zion! Shout in triumph, O daughter of Jerusalem! Behold, your king is coming to you; He is just and endowed with salvation, Humble and mounted on a donkey, Even on a colt, the foal of a donkey.*

He also fulfilled the prophecy given to Daniel by the angel Gabriel that foretold Christ's first coming on the exact day.

As a recap, we are told in Daniel 9:25 that from the time the walls were rebuilt until the coming of the Messiah would be 69 years times 7 years, or 173,880 days (to do the calculation you need to use a 360-day calendar and add the leap years). We read in Nehemiah 2:1–8 that King Artaxerxes signed the decree for Nehemiah to rebuild the city walls on what is calculated to be March 14, 445 BC. (This ancient document can be found in the London Museum today.) If we take March 14, 445 BC, and add 173,880 days, then Christ rode into Jerusalem on April 6th, AD 32. Keep in mind that this was also the first time He let the people receive Him as the Messiah. Before this, He always said, "My time has not yet come" (John 7:6 NKJV), and He hid away from the crowds. The exact day of His coming was arranged, and therefore Christ wept for His people because they did not know their Scriptures. The prophets gave them the exact day, along with how He would enter the city, yet the Jews rejected Him. That is why Christ wept in Luke 19:41, stating, "You did not know the time of your visitation" (Luke 19:44 NKJV).

From that point on, blindness was put on the Jews until the fullness of the Gentiles came (see Romans 11:25). Think about that: Christ wept because His people did not know what His Word had promised. The Creator of the universe arranged the exact day when He would appear, yet no one accepted His Word. Are we guilty of not accepting His Word? The Lord fulfilled the prophecy. The Bible has foretold past, present, and future events, yet are we too caught up in the things of this world to understand that He will come again? We do not know the exact day when He will return, for the Son of Man will come at an hour when we least expect. Woe unto them that do not heed His Word.

"And Jesus said unto them, See ye, not all these things? Verily I say unto you, There shall not be left here one stone upon another, that shall not be thrown down" (Matt. 24:2). Christ started by saying, "See ye, not all these things?" In the Greek language, Christ was saying, "Does it matter? Is this what you think life is about?" Jesus then went on to say that the temple would be destroyed brick by brick. I can imagine that at this point, the disciples whispered among themselves, "How could this be?" Yet, thirty-eight years later, Titus Vespasian, along with his troops of four Roman legions, lay siege to Jerusalem and burned the temple to the ground. In the writings of the historian Josephus (who was an eyewitness to the event), he states that Titus had the soldiers disassemble it brick by brick to retrieve all the gold that was melted between the cracks. Again, our Lord had predicted the future, and it happened exactly as He said it would happen.

> "And as he sat upon the mount of Olives, the disciples came unto him privately, saying, Tell us, when shall these things be? And what Andll be the sign of thy

coming and the end of the world?" (Matt. 24:3). Now we read that Christ sat down on the Mount of Olives, anticipating the disciples' questions. In the Gospel of Mark, we are told that four of the disciples came to Christ privately: Peter, James, John, and Andrew. Keep in mind that it was always Peter, James, and John that the Lord kept close to His heart and revealed many things to (e.g., the transfiguration). Also, notice the Lord predominantly spoke to the multitudes in parables; then later on He would give the disciples a clear and straightforward answer to the parable. So here we have three questions that the disciples asked:

1. *When shall these things be? Or when will the temple be destroyed?*
2. *What shall be the sign of Thy coming?*
3. *What shall be the sign of the end of the world? (This refers to the end of the age or the time of the Gentile rule on Earth.)*

The answer to the first question is given in Luke 21:20: "And when ye shall see Jerusalem compassed with armies, then know that the desolation thereof is nigh." In ancient days, when an army would capture a city, it would camp outside the gates, cut off the food and water supplies to the city, then knock down the city gates and invade. Christ referred to Titus and his army as they were to lay siege to Jerusalem. He also spoke of what the Romans would do to the Jews and their city and how the Jews would be trodden down by the Gentiles: "And they shall fall by the edge of the sword, and shall be led away captive into all nations: and Jerusalem shall be trodden down of the Gentiles until the times of the Gentiles be fulfilled" (Luke 21:24).

Again, history proves this has taken place, and Jerusalem to this day is still not 100 percent under Jewish control; hence, there is no temple. An Islamic mosque sits on the edge of the

Temple Mount near the Dome of the Rock. (According to Jewish law, these temple areas are in perpetuity. But new studies have found the vacant area to the north of these two temples is the rightful place where the new temple will be rebuilt as prophesied in the Scriptures. It will be across from the Gate Beautiful, which is believed to be the gate Christ will re-enter Jerusalem.)

Next, Jesus answered the third question, "When will the end of the age happen?" Our loving Lord started by giving the signs or the seasons of things that must take place before He returns to Earth. Keep in mind that Christ is going to take His Church from the earth (the Rapture) before Hireturnng to Earth to reign and rule.

"And Jesus answered and said unto them, Take heed that no man deceive you. For many shall come in my name, saying, I am Christ; and shall deceive many" (Matt. 24:4–5). Christ said to watch out for false prophets. Satan always sends a counterfeit to deceive the masses. We have seen these counterfeits rise and preach a different gospel. In Revelation 13:13–14, we see the coming of the final false prophet, who is also alluded to in 2 Thessalonians 2:9.

"And ye shall hear of wars and rumors of wars: see that ye be not troubled: for all these things must come to pass, but the end is not yet. For nation shall rise against nation, and kingdom against kingdom" (Matt. 24:6-7). The Lord predicted wars and rumors of wars, yet He said we should not be troubled. Since the Garden of Eden, man has been selfish; it is part of our sinful nature. So the Lord said the man will want and covet things. Yes, there will be fighting and nations rising against nations (wars). This will always be the case until the Lord brings His righteous Kingdom.

"And there shall be famines, and pestilences, and earthquakes, in divers places. All these are the beginning of sorrows" (Matt. 24:7-8). Within the last twenty years, we have seen major earthquakes worldwide; epidemics of disease, such as the AIDS virus in Africa; and tsunamis, such as those that wiped out parts of Indonesia, Thailand, Sri Lanka, and India in December of 2004. (In Indonesia, the night before the tidal wave hit a small Christian village, the Muslim government sent the Christians up into the mountain for their Christmas celebration. When the flood hit, it wiped out the village, but the Christians were spared because they were told to worship their God on the mountain away from the village. It is awesome how the Lord delivers His people from trials and tribulations.)

The Lord warned us that when you see these things, it is just the beginning, like a woman in labor. It starts with a little pain and then really gets intense. "Then shall they deliver you up to be afflicted, and shall kill you: and ye shall be hated of all nations for my name's sake (Matt. 24:9). This statement has a double fulfillment, during the time of the disciples once the Church was established and throughout the ages and in current times. Christians have been persecuted for their faith all over the world throughout history; even today, in Muslim countries, a Christian can be killed for renouncing the Muslim faith and becoming a believer in Jesus Christ.

Some time ago, I was in Beijing, China. When I applied for my visa, I had to sign a waiver stating I would not perform any ministry work. Just think, what if I were to walk into Tiananmen Square and publicly hand out tracts or preach the gospel of Christ? Would I be arrested? Why is it a crime to tell the world about our Lord and Savior who died on the cross and shed His blood so that those who believe in Him can have everlasting life? China is a country with over 1.3 billion people, and three of China's major cities have a population of over 12 million people. Oh, yes, it's true, the harvest is plentiful, yet the laborers are few (Matt. 9:37). Pray for the gospel to become open to the people of that vast country.

"And then shall many be offended, and shall betray one another, and shall hate one another" (Matt. 24:10). This verse also has a double fulfillment. Josephus wrote about how the Jews betrayed each other while the city was under attack, stealing and killing for food; it seems that during the great tribulation, this again will take place.

"And many false prophets shall rise, and shall deceive many" (Matt. 24:11). This we have already addressed. Christ mentioned it three times in this discourse, with an emphasis on false prophets and deception.

"And because iniquity shall abound, the love of many shall wax cold" (Matt. 24:12). Christ spoke about a world full of people who will be focused on themselves with disregard for moral values in a world that is corrupt with pornography, homosexuals and the lust of the flesh, without acknowledging the presence of God.

"But he that shall endure unto the end, the same shall be saved" (Matt. 24:13). This verse also has a double fulfillment. In Revelation 3:10, the Lord spoke to the Church, which will be kept from the hour of tribulation that will be poured out on the earth. Yet I believe that since this chapter of Matthew deals with the Jews in the latter days, this is referring to the 144,000 Jews that are protected by God during the tribulation period. "And this gospel of the kingdom shall be preached in all the world for a witness unto all nations; and then shall the end come" (Matt. 24:14). After the period mentioned in the second chapter of Acts, the Church was established; many of the disciples went throughout the world preaching the gospel (e.g., Paul went to Europe and Asia Minor, and Thomas went to India). Today, thanks to missionaries and the use of the Internet, cable TV, and radio, the gospel has been preached throughout the world. However, the key to this passage is when the Lord said "And then shall the end come." I believe Christ is referring to the angels in Revelation 14:6, "having the everlasting gospel to preach unto them that dwell on the earth, and to every nation, and kindred, and tongue, and people."

In the next few verses, we will notice that the phrasing pertains to people residing in Israel—Jerusalem in particular. "When ye, therefore, shall see the abomination of desolation, spoken of by Daniel the prophet, stand in the holy place, (whoso readeth, let him understand)" (Matt. 24:15). Christ quoted this verse from the Book of Daniel, which was written hundreds of years before Christ was born. This passage is very important because it speaks of the abomination of desolation, which means the temple must be defiled. The exciting part of this is that it implies that Israel will have another temple. According to the Scriptures, the verses relate to a world leader coming to power and bringing peace to Israel and Palestine. He will make a covenant with the nation and rebuild their temple. Ezekiel 40:5 states there will be a wall built between the temple and the outer court (this is where the Dome of the Rock sits).

Continuing, Christ says: "Whoso readeth, let him understand." Wow, pretty heavy! Christ quoted from Daniel and spoke of the temple that will be built, and then He told us to understand and acknowledge this. Yes, at this present time, we are being told to understand this will all take place. Imagine yourself reading this passage in the year 1940. Israelites were not yet in the land, nor had they been for 2,000 years (since about AD 100 or so). There had already been one world war, and another was on the rise. Here in the Scriptures, you read that there will be a temple built in Jerusalem; then Christ states, "Whoso readeth, let him understand."

Today, Israel is back in the land, the European Union has emerged, and a cashless society is about to unfold. Now we can surely understand what our Lord spoke about. How much more evidence do we need? Remember, the Bible was given to us so that we would not be ignorant of the things to come. Our

Lord is coming back—that's a fact! We need to repent now of our sins and trust in His Word.

"For God so loved the world, that he gave his only begotten Son, that whosoever believeth in him should not perish, but have everlasting life" (John 3:16). Yes, Jesus Christ paid the price for our sins so that we could be forgiven. In three days, He rose from the dead and was seen by many, including His disciples. Later most of the disciples died the deaths of martyrs; they each remained strong in their convictions. After seeing the risen Lord, nothing could dissuade them. (Only John, the beloved, did not die a martyr's death; he was banished to the island of Patmos and while there, was given the book of Revelation to write. He was later freed and died of natural causes.) So may I say, "Whoso readeth, let him understand."

In Matthew 24:16–21, Jesus spoke to the people in Israel and gave them instructions on what to do and pray:

> Then let them which be in Judea flee into the mountains: Let him which is on the housetop not come down to take anything out of his house: Neither let him which is in the field return to take his clothes. And woe unto them that are with child, and to them that give suck in those days! But pray ye that your flight is not in the winter, neither on the sabbath day. For then shall be great tribulation, such as was not since the beginning of the world to this time, no, nor ever shall be.

Scripture tells us that after the abomination of desolation happens, God will pour out His judgment on a Christ-rejecting sinful world. The wrath of the Lamb will come down on the whole earth for a three-and-a-half-year period. Then the judgment of God will come, as described in Revelation 6–19. Christ also said that this will be the worst time ever in world history. Just try to imagine worldwide earthquakes;

unfathomable tsunamis; erupting volcanoes; destruction of one-third of the world's population; famine resulting from food and crops being destroyed; nations trying to overpower each other; and hailstones, the size of bricks, falling from the sky. Yes, this will be a time of horror as never been seen before in history; nor will ever be seen again.

Is this fact or fiction? Well, I would not want to speculate. The Lord has been 100 percent accurate thus far. And He has predicted many things that I have seen come to pass in my lifetime. I have also experienced a changed life; old ways were left behind as the Holy Spirit did away with the "wretched, pitiful, poor, blind" person that I was (Rev. 3:17). He has empowered me with a new, born-again nature. I was dead to the things of the Spirit, but I am a new creation in Christ. When Christ takes up residence in your heart, He begins revealing new things through the power of His Holy Spirit.

"And except those days should be shortened, there should no flesh be saved: but for the elect's sake those days shall be shortened" (Matt. 24:22). Our God is loving, and He will always give us a way of escape. During the tribulation, God will show His mercy to the Jews (the elect) and make His return come to pass.

> Then if any man shall say unto you, Lo, here is Christ, or there; believe it not. For there shall arise false Christ and false prophets, and shall shew great signs and wonders; insomuch that, if it were possible, they shall deceive the very elect. Behold, I have told you before. Wherefore if they shall say unto you, Behold, he is in the desert; go not forth: behold, he is in the secret chambers; believe it not" (Matt. 24:23–26).

Again, for the third time, Christ warned about false prophets and false Christ. This must be very important, for Christ to mention it three times in one chapter!

"For as the lightning cometh out of the east, and shineth even unto the west; so shall also the coming of the Son of man be." (Matt. 24:27). Christ says here when He comes, we will know it. The whole earth will see His appearance, so we should not waste our time by looking in other places for the Messiah.

"For wheresoever the carcass is, there will the eagles be gathered together" (Matt. 24:28). Christ spoke here of the battle of Armageddon, found in Revelation 19:17–18.

"Immediately after the tribulation of those days shall the sun be darkened, and the moon shall not give her light, and the stars shall fall from heaven, and the powers of the heavens shall be shaken" (Matt. 24:29). This is a description of a supernova or perhaps the aftermath of nuclear fallout, which could include meteorite showers. A similar passage is found in Revelation 8:12.

"And then shall appear the sign of the Son of man in heaven: and then shall all the tribes of the earth mourn, and they shall see the Son of man coming in the clouds of heaven with power and great glory" (Matt. 24:30). Now we have the glorious appearance of our Lord as He comes in the clouds with His saints (see Revelation 19). We are told in several places in Scripture that the Lord will come in clouds, as He left in Acts 1:9.

"And he shall send his angels with a great sound of a trumpet, and they shall gather together his elect from the four winds, from one end of heaven to the other" (Matt. 24:31). This is a reference to the angels gathering up the remnant of the Jews who come to faith during the tribulation.

"Now learn a parable of the fig tree; When his branch is yet tender and putteth forth leaves, ye know that summer is nigh: So likewise ye, when ye shall see all these things, know that it is near, even at the doors" (Matt. 24:32–33). Christ told this parable relating Israel to a fig tree, saying that when Israel is back in the land, we will know the time is getting closer. Israel has returned to the land and is a nation again, after over 2,000 years. This all took place on May 14, 1948. Israel is the only country to become a nation on an exact date. This exact date was prophesied by Daniel.

"Verily I say unto you, this generation shall not pass, till all these things be fulfilled" (Matt. 24:34). The Greek word translated generation in this verse can refer to a race of people, so this could be what Christ spoke of. Keep in mind that many have tried to wipe out the Jews, from Haman (in the book of Esther) to Hitler. Yet the Lord has protected and preserved them. This generation could also refer to the people who see these things come to pass (e.g., Israel's return to the land, the rise of the European nations, a cashless society, and so on.) Either way, we are currently living in a time when these prophecies are being fulfilled. Do not lose sight of the fact that Christ told us in advance to keep an eye out for the seasons and the time in which we live. The tree is blossoming, and the fruit will soon appear.

"Heaven and earth shall pass away, but my words shall not pass away" (Matt. 24:35). In Revelation 21, we read of a new heaven and a new earth. Christ referred to old things passing away, while His Word promises a new beginning.

"But of that day and hour knoweth no man; no, not the angels of heaven, but my Father only" (Matt. 24:36). Only the Father knows when Jesus will return. This is referred to as the Blessed Hope, which is when Christ returns to rapture His saints. We are told in Daniel the exact time when Christ will return to the earth to rule and reign (1,290 years after the abomination of desolation). Still, no one knows when He will return to meet us in the clouds. We know from Romans 11:25 that we are waiting for the fullness of the Gentiles to come in before Christ will remove His Church and deal with the nation of Israel again.

Because God is omniscient, knowing all from beginning to end, He also knows the exact number of people chosen to join the elect in Christ. When that number is finally reached, the Rapture will happen. With the world in its present state of chaos and so many prophecies being fulfilled, it is necessary for us, the elect, to get the gospel to as many lost souls as possible.

> *But as the days of Noah were, so shall also the coming of the Son of man be. For as in the days that were before the flood they were eating and drinking, marrying and giving in marriage, until the day that Noah entered into the ark, And knew not until the flood came, and took them all away; so shall also the coming of the Son of man be (Matt. 24:37–39).*

The days of Noah were so corrupt that God had to intercede with a worldwide flood and cleanse the earth of its wickedness. Yet our Lord is a loving God, and He always provides the righteous a way out of judgment. Noah preached repentance for 120 years while he was building the ark. People enjoyed mocking Noah and making fun of him. They refused to believe the warning of God—and the flood came. The Bible tells us that in the days of Noah, there were homosexuals and people worshipping images; they had no sense of any morals. The people did just as they liked, and God judged them based on their choices. The Lord said that as the days of Noah were, so it will be when the Son of man returns. The times we are living in now seem to be even worse than the days of Noah. People's sinful natures have not changed; they still have the same sinful hearts. Due to today's modern technology, we can bring even more immoral values into our homes. Between what is broadcast on TV (sex, violence, murders, physical abuse, and so on) and what is seen on the Internet, this generation has far more opportunities than in Noah's time.

Also note that Christ said, "They knew not until the flood came." Christ was aware they would not believe, as their hearts had already grown cold. But, because of His loving nature, He gave them an opportunity and had Noah preach repentance for all those years; yet the people wanted to live their lives their way, choosing the pleasures of this world over God's invitation to eternal salvation. So will it be when the Son of man returns? Will we hearken to His Word? Hasn't Christ given us enough forewarning? World history has given us all the evidence we need. Yes, He is coming! How will you respond? You are either for Him or against Him; there is no middle ground. He has given us His Holy Spirit to convict us of these things. Each of us will be held accountable for what we know. On Judgment Day, the only question that will be asked of us is, "What did you do with My Son?" Accept Him, or reject Him? And this is what we will be held accountable for.

"Then shall two be in the field; the one shall be taken, and the other left. Two women shall be grinding at the mill; the one shall be taken, and the other left" (Matt. 24:40–41). These verses speak of the Rapture of the Church and how some will be taken and others will be left behind. See 1 Corinthians 15:51–55 and 1 Thessalonians 4:16–18 for more information.

> *Watch, therefore: for ye know not what hour your Lord doth come. But know this, that if the goodman of the house had known in what watch the thief would come, he would have watched, and would not have suffered his house to be broken up. Therefore be ye also ready: for in such an hour as ye think not the Son of man cometh (Matt. 24:42–44).*

Therefore be ready at all times. In everything you do, anticipate that Christ could come any minute.

"Who then is a faithful and wise servant, whom his lord hath made ruler over his household, to give them meat in due season?" (Matt. 24:45). Again, the Lord told us that the ones who are wise and follow His words will receive the rewards.

"Blessed is that servant, whom his lord when he cometh shall find so doing. Verily I say unto you, that he shall make him ruler over all his goods" (Matt. 24:46–47). Blessed is he who obeys the great Master, for he will inherit the Kingdom. For the Lord will say, "Well done, good and faithful servant" (Matt. 25:23).

> But and if that evil servant shall say in his heart, My lord delayeth his coming; And shall begin to smite his fellow servants, and to eat and drink with the drunken; The lord of that servant shall come in a day when he looketh not for him, and in an hour that he is not aware of, And shall cut him asunder, and appoint him his portion with the hypocrites: there shall be weeping and gnashing of teeth (Matt. 24:48–51).

This is an interesting statement because it speaks of someone who knows the Master, His ways, words, and whereabouts, yet in his heart denies the truth. In Revelation 3:14–20, Christ spoke to the lukewarm church. That is the church that thought it knew the Lord but did not abide in Him. The Lord stated, "Because you are lukewarm, and neither cold nor hot, I will vomit you out of my mouth" (Revelation 3:16 NKJV). In other words, Jesus would rather you did not know Him than have you pretend that you are part of His family. These are the people that know His Word but do what is right in their own eyes. They set up their doctrine within the Church and preach and live a different gospel.

Christ said to the Church, "Behold, I stand at the door and knock. If anyone hears My voice and opens the door, I will come into him and dine with him, and he with Me" (Revelation

3:20 NKJV). Christ desires to be close and personal. Yet many of today's churches do not recognize that He is alive and just waiting for them to open the doors of their hearts. These are the churchgoers who will miss the Rapture because they did not believe or receive Christ into their hearts or prepare themselves for His coming again. To them, it will be like the days of Noah! Eating, drinking, and going about their lives until the Son of man returns for His Church and gives these hypocrites over to the pleasures of their flesh. And then there shall be weeping and gnashing of teeth for all who have not repented of their sins. "He that hath an ear, let him hear what the Spirit saith unto the churches" (Rev. 3:22)!

Matthew Chapter 24 - Timeline

Triumphal Entry

CHRIST ENTERS
JERUSALEM
PALM SUNDAY.

Christ Predicts the
destruction of the Temple.

CHRIST
ON OR ABOUT THE
9TH OF NISIAN
LEAVES THE TEMPLE
FOR THE LAST TIME!

OLIVIT DISCOURSE

CHRIST GIVES THE
DISCIPLES AN
OVERVIEW OF
THINGS THAT WILL
HAPPEN IN THE
LATER DAYS.

CHRIST CRUCIFIED

CHRIST CRUCIFIED ON THE 14TH OF
NISIAN AND AROSE AGAIN ON THE 17TH.

TEMPLE DESTROYED

70 AD TITUS VISPASIAN AND THE 7th
LEGEND TAKE JERUSALEM AND DESTROYS
THE TEMPLE.

Chapter 6:
The Unveiling—"The Coming of the Antichrist"

Imagine a world in perfect peace. No wars or famines, complete economic prosperity, one-world government, one-world religion, one-world monetary system, and the perfect world leader. A man who unites countries, leaders, and religions and generates world peace. A charismatic man who wins the world over. Elegant in speech, bold, powerful, and able to execute plans. The perfect world leader! Yes, the man with a plan; he has all the right answers and can charm all. Could there be such a man? Would the world embrace him? Let's take a look at what the Bible has to say about this coming world leader. Where does he come from? What is his nature? What will he accomplish? And how will he come to power?

The Time: The twenty-first century.

The Place: Brussels.

The Players: Ten United countries (the United Community of Europe and nine other nations).

They join together to elect a one-world government, to be governed by a charismatic politician who has gained the world's trust and now is elected as the president of this newly established government. His charm, power, and demeanor make him the hands-down candidate for this new position. Of European descent, this charismatic man ushers in his reign by confirming a treaty with Israel to rebuild their temple upon the Temple Mount. This treaty includes building a wall between the Dome of the Rock Mosque and the new temple. This then gives the Jews their temple in which to re-establish the ritual sacrifices, all the while leaving the outer court, divided by this new wall so that the Muslims can hold their worship. The Jews hail this charismatic man as a messiah and "worship" him for bringing peace and their sacrifices back. (The beautiful one-of-a-kind temple was destroyed in AD 70 by Titus and the Roman legion; since then the Jews have had no temple in which to hold sacrifices).

Next, this world leader brings in a one-world monetary system and issues in a cashless society. He immediately chooses a spiritual leader who unites all religions, and this ends the religious conflict, bringing peace and harmony among religious leaders. During his reign, an assassination attempt is made on his life; he loses the use of his arm and right eye and is left for dead. But he makes a miraculous recovery and performs supernatural miracles. The world marvels over his powers, wisdom, and ability to survive and execute his plans. The stock market is booming. Peace, harmony, and a joyful atmosphere spread throughout all the nations. Iraq becomes the trade center of the Middle East, and businesses become exceedingly prosperous.

One day this world leader organizes a press conference to be broadcast worldwide from the Temple Mount. It will be at midday in Jerusalem. CNN, the BBC and all the other world networks are there. The cameras are set up inside the temple and aimed toward the podium. This charismatic leader then makes his public announcement to the world, claiming he is "God" and demanding that the world worship him. He curses the true and living God and blasphemes God's name. The world is in uproar! This charismatic leader seemed to be the answer to the world's problems but now is showing his true nature.

Nations of the world will begin mustering their strength to overthrow the leader's government. The kings of the east will march with 200 million soldiers, uniting with various other nations, and the Antichrist will have to retreat to Israel due to these nations coming up against him. The setting now moves to the Valley of Megiddo, where the last world war is to take place. At just the right moment, out of the clouds will come our Lord and Savior, Jesus Christ, with His saints, and He will supernaturally intercede. The Lord will set foot on the Mount of Olives as it splits in two with a great earthquake. He will destroy the armies of the world with His glorious appearance and the power of the Word of God.

Now let's take the time to look into more details regarding these events and the Bible passages that expound on them. Because so much of this sounds like fiction or a dream scene, it is important to start with some background about this charismatic leader, and what the Bible says about him. Next, "the day of the Lord" will be covered—the Second Advent! And finally, what is preventing the Antichrist from coming to power?

His Name

The last world leader is referred to throughout the Bible. He has various names, including "the prince that shall come" (Dan. 9:26); "the idol shepherd" (Zech. 11:17); "that man of sin" and "the son of perdition" (2 Thess. 2:3); and "the lawless one" (2 Thess. 2:8–9 NKJV). In the book of Revelation, he is called the "Beast" and the "Antichrist," and he is referred to as the "horn" in the books of Daniel and Revelation.

"Little children, it is the last time: and as ye have heard that antichrist shall come, even now are there many antichrists; whereby we know that it is the last time" (1 John 2:18). In this verse, John was warning the people (little children referred to new believers in Christ) that there are already evil leaders at work, but in the end, times will come to a final antichrist. Interestingly, John is the only writer that refers to him as the Antichrist.

Where He Comes From

And whereas thou sawest the feet and toes, part of potters' clay, and part of iron, the kingdom shall be divided; but there shall be in it of the strength of the iron, forasmuch as thou sawest the iron mixed with miry clay. And as the toes of the feet were part of iron, and part of clay, so the kingdom shall be partly strong, and partly broken. And whereas thou sawest iron mixed with miry clay, they shall mingle themselves with the seed of men: but they shall not cleave one to another, even as iron is not mixed with clay (Dan. 2:41–43).

These verses speak of how this world leader will come out of the divided Roman empire, with stronger and weaker nations joining together to become one. Once this world leader shows his true power, the nations will come against him (leading to the final battle in the Valley of Megiddo).

History shows that the Roman Empire was never conquered but fell apart from within (e.g., a civil war). Daniel tells us that the legs of iron represent the division of the empire, and it shows how in the end times the empire will come back together. We have already seen Europe unite (smaller and weaker nations joining together), so from the text, we believe that this world leader will come out of the European community or be of Roman descent. The passage in Daniel could also refer to the European community uniting with other nations (nine more) and becoming strong. We do know from the text that the Roman Empire was divided, with one division returning to Europe while the other migrated down to Assyria.

About the Lawless One

> *And his power shall be mighty, but not by his power: and he shall destroy wonderfully, and shall prosper, and practice, and shall destroy the mighty and the holy people. And through his policy also he shall cause craft to prosper in his hand, and he shall magnify himself in his heart, and by peace shall destroy many: he shall also stand up against the Prince of princes, but he shall be broken without hand" (Dan. 8:24–25).*

This passage in Daniel describes the world leader as mighty, with powers not his own. This is speaking of him being empowered by Satan. Satan will give this man the power to perform miracles and awesome feats that amaze the world. There will be prosperity for a time. Then our Lord Jesus Christ will prevail and overpower Satan and his hosts at the end!

"And in his estate shall stand up a vile person, to whom they shall not give the honor of the kingdom: but he shall come in peaceably, and obtain the kingdom by flatteries" (Dan. 11:21). Here it speaks of the leader coming in as a peacemaker and obtaining control with his manipulations; yet after his initial campaign, the world will see his false "truth."

Temple Predictions

> *And he shall confirm the covenant with many for one week: and amid the week he shall cause the sacrifice and the oblation to cease, and for the overspreading of abominations he shall make it desolate, even until the consummation, and that determined shall be poured upon the desolate (Dan. 9:27).*

In this passage, one week refers to seven years, during which the world leader will confirm a treaty with Israel and encourage the rebuilding of the temple. But amid the week (after three and a half years), he will broadcast throughout the world and demand to be worshiped.

"When yet, therefore, shall see the abomination of desolation, spoken of by Daniel the prophet, stand in the holy place, (whoso readeth, let him understand:)" (Matt. 24:15). Here Christ is quoting Daniel and asking the reader to understand what will happen in the future. Our Lord God is loving, and He does not want any to perish. He gives us His Holy Spirit to convict our hearts of our sins, and He gives us His written Word to show us all things. He is the creator of this universe, and with Him all things are possible. "In the beginning, God created the heaven and the earth" (Gen. 1:1).

God is "the Alpha and the Omega, the First and the Last" (Rev. 1:11); and He sent His only Son, Jesus Christ, to walk among us. He died for our sins so that through His resurrection we could live forever.

"And from the time that the daily sacrifice shall be taken away, and the abomination that maketh desolate set up, there shall be a thousand two hundred and ninety days" (Dan. 12:11). This again is referring to the second half of the seven years, and this is where God pours out His wrath on a Christ-rejecting sinful world (see Revelation 6 to 19).

> And behold a wall on the outside of the house round about, and in the man's hand a measuring reed of six cubits long by the cubit and a hand breadth: so he measured the breadth of the building, one reed; and the height, one reed. Then came he unto the gate which looketh toward the east, and went up the stairs thereof, and measured the threshold of the gate, which was one reed broad; and the other threshold of the gate, which was one reed broad (Ezek. 40:5,6).

Then he measured the breadth from the forefront of the lower gate unto the forefront of the inner court without, a hundred cubits eastward and northward (Ezek. 40:19).

In these verses, Ezekiel speaks of the wall that will be put up to divide the new temple and the outer court. The wall is said to be about six cubits (18 feet) high and a hundred cubits (300 feet) long.

"But the court which is without the temple leave out, and measure it not; for it is given unto the Gentiles: and the holy city shall they tread under foot forty and two months" (Rev. 11:2). Here in Revelation we are told that the outer court (or outside the wall) is given to the Gentiles; this is where the Dome of the Rock Mosque sits. So the temple will be divided by a wall that separates the Jewish and the Muslim worship centers. Also notice again the reference to forty-two months, or three and a half years, during which there are troublesome times.

Assassination Attempt

"Woe to the idol shepherd that leaveth the flock! The sword shall be upon his arm, and his right eye: his arm shall be clean dried up, and his right eye shall be utterly darkened" (Zech. 11:17). In Zechariah we read of this idol shepherd (one of the names for the world leader) who has an assassination attempt on his life that leaves him with the loss of an arm and his right eye.

"And causeth the earth and them which dwell therein to worship the first beast, whose deadly wound was healed (Rev. 13:12). This idol shepherd's deadly wound is healed. And the world marvels over his recovery. (Take a close look at how specific the Bible is in describing in detail all that will take place in the future.)

Mark of the Beast

> *And he causeth all, both small and great, rich and poor, free and bond, to receive a mark in their right hand, or their foreheads: And that no man might buy or sell, save he that had the mark, or the name of the beast, or the number of his name. Here is wisdom. Let him that hath understanding count the number of the beast: for it is the number of a man, and the number is Six hundred three score and six (Rev. 13:16–18).*

As this book is being written in AD 2008, this technology is in place, ready to be implemented but still on hold! When I am preaching and teaching on this subject, I read these verses from a reprint of an AD 1620 publication of the Bible. Yes! Nearly 400 years ago this Bible was in print, and even then it foretold a cashless society in which no one—small or great, rich or poor—will be able to buy or sell without taking a mark on their right hand or forehead. The New Testament was written nearly 2,000 years ago, and it is amazing how accurate it is regarding past, present, and future events, including detailed descriptions. Yes! Past events have been accurately prophesied and fulfilled; therefore expect prophecies of future events to be just as accurate! Many technologies mentioned in the Scriptures are on the horizon and soon to be part of our lives.

Fifty years ago, we could never imagine any of this taking place. However, in this day and age, how could one dispute the fact that we are heading towards a cashless society or a nuclear war, or a one-world leader? In the United States, one of the local banks runs a TV commercial that shows a bank teller scanning a man's forehead. In our local supermarkets, we now have a new technology called U-Scan-It. This system gives the consumer the option of bypassing a store clerk and the lines of people and going directly to this self-serve technology. We can weigh our produce by scanning the product key on the fruit, and the machine calculates the weight and price. Amazing!

Getting back to this verse in Revelation, keep in mind the key point—he causes all to take the mark. It is believed that this cashless society will be in place before the world leader's coming. Perhaps when this technology is approved by the government it may be more of a convenience for upper and middle-class societies. Again I stress the importance of this verse emphasizing the fact that this world leader will make it mandatory to take his mark, or else be put to death.

The next part of this prophecy speaks of a number given to this man. That number is 666. In this present day, we do not understand what this represents (other than knowing that it is Satan's number and mark, which is a reference to his demonic powers). The passage goes on to relate that there will be those during this period who have knowledge and wisdom relating to all that is happening. (It may be the lukewarm Christians who miss the Rapture, because, although they have exposure to the Bible, they never take it seriously.) They may recognize what this is all about and who this person is. But true believers in Christ will not be here to experience these horrific events, for the Bible says He will keep us from the tribulation that will fall upon the earth. We are not looking for the Antichrist. We are looking for our Blessed Hope, our Lord, and Savior Jesus Christ, who is the only One to shed His blood so we can have everlasting life. The Lord of lords and King of kings will come and save us from an hour of tribulation that this world has never seen before. Blessed be His Holy name. Amen!

Worshipping the Beast and Blasphemies

And they worshipped the dragon which gave power unto the beast: and they worshipped the beast, saying, Who is like unto the beast? Who can make war with him? And there was given unto him a mouth speaking great things and blasphemies and was given unto him to continue forty and two months. And he opened his mouth in blasphemy against God, to blaspheme his name, and his tabernacle, and them that dwell in heaven (Rev. 13:4–6).

Here we read that Satan gives power to this world leader, and many in the world worship him. We also read that he is given the authority to rule for forty-two months. Then, because of ego and stupidity, he speaks blasphemy and curses God.

In this passage, we have Satan empowering the world leader. At the same time, God releases to him the authority to go about his business for three and a half years. (If this sounds strange to you, then perhaps you should read the book of Job to get a better understanding of the dialogue between God and Satan. You will find that God does let Satan have power over the earth.) But God will only let Satan do so much.

Keep in mind that Adam forfeited the title deed to the earth in the Garden of Eden. Therefore, after the forty-two months of "Satanic rule," our Lord Jesus Christ redeems (or claims back) the title deed during His millennial reign on Earth. (See Revelation 20 for more details).

I beheld then because of the voice of the great words which the horn spake: I beheld even till the beast was slain, and his body destroyed and given to the burning flame (Dan. 7:11).

And he shall speak great words against the highest, and shall wear out the saints of the highest, and think to change times and laws: and they shall be given into his hand until a time and times and the dividing of time (Dan. 7:25).

And the king shall do according to his will, and he shall exalt himself, and magnify himself above every god, and shall speak marvelous things against the God of gods, and shall prosper till the indignation be accomplished: for that, that is determined shall be done (Dan. 11:36).

Daniels relates how this world leader will speak words against the Highest God and try to exalt himself as a god. And Daniel 7:25 states he will try to change times and laws. Let's take a closer look at these passages.

In the United States, our forefathers founded this country and based our constitution on the Ten Commandments, although nowadays we see that these principles are fading away. Keeping this in mind, we would assume that these passages refer to the world leader making his global law or constitution and making changes in the time and date system. Could it be because each time we sign a document we acknowledge the year of our Lord? That's right. Nearly 2,000 years ago, a man named Jesus walked the earth among men and women; and since then, our dating system affirms that He did live and die here on earth. Could this be the reason why this world leader will declare his own time and date system? Be prepared; Satan plans to do away with any mention of our Lord. (The only thing that says "In God We Trust" is our currency. I believe that there will not be any issue with taking God off our currency, because the cashless society will just do away with currency altogether.)

Armies against Him

And at the time of the end shall the king of the south push at him: and the king of the north shall come against him like a whirlwind, with chariots, and with horsemen, and with many ships; and he shall enter into the countries, and shall overflow and pass over. He shall enter also into the glorious land, and many countries shall be overthrown: but these shall escape out of his hand, even Edom, and Moab, and the chief of the children of Ammon. He shall stretch forth his hand also upon the countries: and the land of Egypt shall not escape. But he shall have power over the treasures of gold and of silver, and over all the precious things of Egypt: and the Libyans and the Ethiopians shall be at his steps. But tidings out of the east and out of the north shall trouble him: therefore he shall go forth with great fury to destroy and utterly make away many. And he shall plant the tabernacles of his palace between the seas in the glorious holy mountain; yet he shall come to his end, and none shall help him (Dan. 11:40–45).

This passage speaks of the countries that come up against the leader during the last half of his reign. This is what leads up to the battle of Armageddon. He sets out to battle, but news from the east has him retreat to protect his position.

Armageddon and the Second Advent

In the following passages in Revelation, Daniel and Zechariah speak of the gathering of the armies of the world that set out to overcome the world leader and his men. But the Lord intercedes. This is referred to as the Battle of Armageddon.

And he gathered them together into a place called in the Hebrew tongue Armageddon (Rev. 16:16).

And I saw the beast, and the kings of the earth, and their armies, gathered together to make war against him that sat on the horse, and against his army" (Rev. 19:19).

I beheld, and the same horn made war with the saints and prevailed against them; Until the Ancient of days came, and judgment was given to the saints of the highest; and the time came that the saints possessed the kingdom (Dan. 7:21–22).

Then shall the LORD go forth, and fight against those nations, as when he fought in the day of battle. And his feet shall stand in that day upon the mount of Olives, which is before Jerusalem on the east, and the mount of Olives shall cleave in the midst thereof toward the east and the west, and there shall be a very great valley, and half of the mountain shall remove toward the north and half of it toward the south. And ye shall flee to the valley of the mountains; for the valley of the mountains shall reach unto Azal: yea, ye shall flee, like as ye fled from before the earthquake in the days of Uzziah king of Judah: and the LORD my God shall come, and all the saints with thee (Zech 14:3–5).

And I saw heaven opened, and behold a white horse, and he that sat upon him was called Faithful and True, and in righteousness, he doth judge and make war. His eyes were as a flame of fire, and on his head were many crowns, and he had a name written, that no man knew, but he was clothed with a vesture dipped in blood: and his name is called The Word of God. And the armies which were in heaven followed him upon white horses, clothed in fine linen, white and clean. And out of his mouth goeth a sharp sword, that with it he should smite the nations: and he shall rule them with a rod of iron: and he treadeth the winepress of the fierceness and wrath of Almighty God. And he hath on his vesture and his thigh a name is written, KING OF KINGS, AND LORD OF LORDS (Rev. 19:11–16).

All of the above verses, in both the Old and New Testament, are referring to the Second Advent, when Christ comes with His bride (the Church) to wipe out the armies of the world.

Withholding Force

The Bible has given us a detailed description of this world leader, such as where he will come from, what his nature will be, and so on. So the big question is, where is he now? When will he come to power? As stated earlier, we, as Christians, are not looking for the Antichrist. We are waiting for our Blessed Hope, the appearance of our Lord and Savior, Jesus Christ, coming to receive His bride (the Church).

"Let no man deceive you by any means: for that day shall not come, except there comes a falling away first, and that man of sin be revealed, the son of perdition" (2 Thess. 2:3). This verse and the next several verses speak about this man of sin is at work yet not revealed. According to the Bible, two things must happen before this leader will come to power. Let's take a look!

The first prerequisite is a falling away or an apostasy of the faith. The root word is apostasy in Greek, which means "to depart from" or "the removal of." This refers to people becoming worldly and being concerned with themselves and not acknowledging God. Look at the world today compared to fifty years ago. What happened to our morals and our standards? Things we see exploited today (e.g., homosexuality and pornography) would make one think, "What is this world coming to?" The number falling away from the faith has been rapidly increasing, and one has to wonder, how much more of it will the Lord stand for?

"And now ye know what withholdeth that he might be revealed in his time. For the mystery of iniquity doth already work: only he whom now letteth will let until he rose out of the way" (2 Thess. 2:6–7). We read that this world leader is already at work yet being held back. We are told in Scripture that the restraining force is the Body of Christ or the Holy Spirit within the believers. Therefore, we, the Church, must be removed from the earth before this leader can come to power (i.e., the Rapture of the church—the second prerequisite).

Although the Lord spoke this universe into existence and gave us DNA as proof that there is a creator, people still seem to disregard the truth. For He said, "I am the resurrection and the life; he who believes in Me will live even if he dies, and everyone who lives and believes in Me will never die" (John 11:25–26, NASB). Christ is the first and the last, the alpha and omega, and only through Christ can we receive everlasting life. We, the Body of Christ, are the restraining force, and once we are taken out, the world leader will be revealed.

> *And I saw when the Lamb opened one of the seals, and I heard, as it were the noise of thunder, one of the four beasts saying, come and see. And I saw, and behold a white horse: and he that sat on him had a bow; and, the drone was given unto him: and he went forth conquering, and to conquer (Rev. 6:1–2).*

These verses show the world leader coming on the scene after the Church has been removed. Then the rider on the white horse comes into power. Keep in mind, Jesus Christ also appears on a white horse, in Revelation 19. But this white horse rider is the Antichrist who comes in as a "peaceful savior."

> *And then shall that Wicked be revealed, whom the Lord shall consume with the spirit of his mouth, and shall destroy with the brightness of his coming: Even him, whose coming is after the working of Satan with all power and signs and lying wonders, And with all deceivableness of unrighteousness in them that perish; because they received not the love of the truth, that they might be saved. And for this cause, God shall send them strong delusion, that they should believe a lie: That they all might be damned who believed not the truth, but had*

pleasure in unrighteousness. But we are bound to give thanks always to God for you, brethren beloved of the Lord, because God hath from the beginning chosen you to salvation through sanctification of the Spirit and belief of the truth (2 Thess. 2:8–13).

This passage jumps ahead seven years to when the Lord will consume this world leader with His Word (the Spirit of truth). This event takes place at the end of the battle of Armageddon. Then the Lord speaks of all those who rejected His Spirit and are unrighteous, who received not the love of the truth. The Scriptures convey that God will send a strong deluding influence so that the people of the world will believe the lie (that is, the words and beliefs of the world leader) and will accept, follow, and worship this leader.

Again, if this sounds strange, refer back to the Old Testament writings and look at Moses and Pharaoh. The Lord told Moses He would harden Pharaoh's heart so he would not let Moses and God's people leave Egypt. The final plague that took the life of Pharaoh's son initiated the release of the Israelites, and Pharaoh then pursued them to the Red Sea, where the Lord protected His people and wiped out their enemies!

Joel 1:15 says, "Alas for the day! For the day of the LORD is at hand. "Then 1 Thessalonians 5:2 reminds us that "The day of the Lord so cometh as a thief in the night." Yet the scoffers say, "Where is He?" "When is He coming?"(see 2 Peter 3:4). We are told in 2 Peter 2:9 that the Lord knows how to deliver His people. The Bible teaches us that we cannot serve two masters (Matt. 6:24). We are either for Him or against Him— there is no in-between ground (Matt. 12:20). Will you be waiting for Jesus Christ, or will you embrace the Antichrist? "He who has an ear let him hear."

The Coming of Our Lord

We pray, "Thy Kingdom come, Thy will be done on earth as it is in heaven." This is His promise. The Bible is God's way of communicating with us. We can understand His nature, love, and, plan for His people. The Lord has laid out a road map to eternal life. He was given us physical evidence by predicting the past, the present, and the future. More importantly, He has given us His Holy Spirit to guide us throughout our lives. We are held accountable for what we know, and when it comes time for the final judgment the only question we will be faced with is, "What did you do with My Son?" As stated earlier, you are either for Him or against Him—there is no middle ground. To know Christ is to accept Him, confess your sins to Him, trust in Him, and live a life of anticipation that He is coming at any moment!

Chapter 7:
Babylon in Prophecy

Babylon is mentioned over 300 times in the Bible, and it is the same Babylon that you read about in today's newspapers and hear about in the news. In the book of Revelation, it is depicted in two different ways. First is the Mystery Babylon, which refers to the secular, commercial way of the world system. Secondly is the literal Babylon, which today is known as Baghdad.

This great city was founded by the first world dictator— Nimrod (the great-grandson of Noah). Tradition pictures him as an impious tyrant who built the Tower of Babel. Babylon is a literal city on the banks of the Euphrates and at one time was known for its hanging gardens. These gardens were so magnificent that they were one of the Seven Wonders of the Ancient World.

Nebuchadnezzar prided himself on the greatness of this city. (See the book of Daniel.) In 1987 Saddam Hussein spent hundreds of millions of dollars on the restoration of the city. One of his greatest challenges was to bring back its ancient treasures, which are still held in museums around the world. One sought-after treasure is the great Ishtar Gate, located in the Berlin Museum. This great gate is a true museum tourist attraction. (A German expedition dismantled the upper level of the Gate of Ishtar in 1902. Then they transported it to Berlin, along with 118 of the 120 friezes of lions from the sides of Nebuchadnezzar's Procession Street.)

The Bible speaks of the fall of Babylon. It was conquered by the Medes and the Persians in 539 BC. It served as a secondary capital of the Persian Empire for over two centuries until Alexander the Great, and then it was conquered by Persia in 325 BC. Alexander the Great went on to make this uniquely beautiful city his capital; he ruled from there until he died in his early thirties.

In the latter days, we are told, Babylon will again be a great commerce center for the Middle East. This is interesting, because, for the last twenty-five years or so, Iraq was under the dictatorship of Saddam Hussein. Yet, today we are seeing the United Nations, led by the United States, moving towards democracy in this land. This may be the genesis for the regrouping of the nation and the open-door scenario. Keep in mind that Iraq is endowed with great oil reserves. The Bible prophecies declare that Babylon will be a mega commercial city in the world of business.

It is also interesting to note that the book of Ezekiel (chapter 38) speaks of nations that will come up against Israel in the last few days, but Iraq is not mentioned in this prophecy. When reading Ezekiel before the fall of Saddam Hussein in 2003, many people questioned why Iraq would be omitted from the prophecy.

The Bible states that Babylon's destruction will cause the merchants of the world to weep (Rev. 18:9–11). The prophecies are that the city will be utterly wiped out in one hour (as if a nuclear bomb were unleashed on it), and the merchants of the world will stand afar off:

"The merchants of these things, who became rich from her, will stand at a distance because of the fear of her torment, weeping and mourning, saying, 'Woe, woe, the great city, she who was clothed in fine linen and purple and scarlet, and adorned with gold and precious stones and pearls; for in one hour such great wealth has been laid waste!' And every shipmaster and every passenger and sailor, and as many as make their living by the sea, stood at a distance, and were crying out as they saw the smoke of her burning, saying, 'What city is like the great city?'" (Rev. 18:15–18 NASB).

This is truly an astonishing prophecy. As always, it is interesting to see God at work with a plan documented throughout His written Word—the Holy Bible. He has laid out the world's history and the things to come with such precision and accuracy! The Lord declares that He knows everything from beginning to end, and so far, everything stated in the Holy Bible has been proven true repeatedly. God has given us advance notice in His Word so we may know He is "the way, and the truth, and the life; no one comes to the Father but through Me" (John 14:6 NASB). It's true! He is the Begotten Son of God, The Lord, the one and only loving God who was at the beginning and will be at the end. So look up, stay alert and prepared, for "the day of the LORD is near" (Joel 1:15 NASB).

THE
LAST
DAYS

Chapter 8:
The Last Days

Israel in Prophecy

The setting: Israel in the twenty-first century. The headline read "Tension in the Middle East." The players, Iran, Turkey, Libya, Ethiopia, and the southern regions of what was once the Soviet Union, have set their sights to attack Israel! Israel seems to be against all odds and hopeless, yet they overcome their attackers! How can this be? This small country, the thorn in the Middle East, has defeated the Muslim nations that have come up against it. "Impossible," you might say! Yet this is what the Bible predicts will happen, for the Lord states from that day forward the house of Israel will know that He is their God.

"Interesting," you might say. Well, let's take a look at what the God of the universe has to say about this battle against His people. We start in Ezekiel 38, where God gives a vision to Ezekiel regarding which nations will be in this battle and what will take place. Keep in mind that Ezekiel was written around the year 589 BC. Islam was not established until around AD 300, yet all of these countries described in this chapter are Islamic nations! Let's get started!

> *"The word of the LORD came to me: "Son of man, set your face against Gog, of the land of Magog, the chief prince of Meshech and Tubal; prophesy against him and say: 'This is what the Sovereign LORD says: I am against*

you, O Gog, chief prince of Meshech and Tubal'" (Ezek. 38:1–3 NIV).

The Lord gave Ezekiel a vision. Gog is the chief prince or leader of the land of Magog (which represents the former Soviet Union and its southern regions), and Meshech represents Moscow and Tubal (historical maps do not clearly state which city this is).

> *And I will turn thee back, and put hooks into thy jaws, and I will bring thee forth, and all thine army, horses and horsemen, all of them clothed with all sorts of armor, even a great company with bucklers and shields, all of them handling swords (Ezek. 38:4).*

Ezekiel is describing weapons of warfare that were used in his day. If this were modern-day writing, perhaps the writer might have used words such as tanks and Apache helicopters, etc.

> *"Persia, Cush, and Put will be with them, all with shields and helmets, also Gomer with all its troops, and Beth Togarmah from the far north with all its troops— the many nations with you. Get ready; be prepared, you and all the hordes gathered about you, and take command of them" (Ezek. 38:5–7 NIV).*

First look at where these nations in the Bible came from. In Genesis 10 we are given a genealogy of the descendants of Noah and where they settled. Keeping this in mind, we can then take ancient-day maps and place them next to the maps of today to get a better understanding of who these nations are.

Genesis–Genealogy

> *Now these are the generations of the sons of Noah, Shem, Ham, and Japheth: and unto them were sons born after the flood. The sons of Japheth; Gomer, Magog,*

Madai, Javan, Tubal, Meshech, and Tiras. And the sons of Gomer; Ashkenaz, Riphath, and Togarmah. And the sons of Javan; Elishah, Tarshish, Kittim, and Dodanim. By these were the isles of the Gentiles divided into their lands everyone after his tongue, after their families, in their nations. And the sons of Ham; Cush, Mizraim, Phut, and Canaan. And the sons of Cush; Seba, Havilah, Sabtah, Raamah, and Sabtechah: and the sons of Raamah; Sheba, and Dedan. And Cush begat Nimrod: he began to be a mighty one in the earth (Gen. 10:1–8).

Let's take a look at who these nations represent in today's world:

Magog = Russia and its southern regions Persia = Iran

Cush = Ethiopia Put = Libya

Gomer = Countries north of Turkey Togarmah = Turkey

(Note: Out of Magog came the Scythians in the seventh century who brought about the rise of Islam.)

Let's also take a look at the names of countries surrounding Israel that are not mentioned in this battle:

1) Egypt
2) Jordon
3) Syria
4) Iraq

This is very interesting, especially Iraq not being mentioned. Before the fall of Saddam Hussein, it was very hard to read this verse and reason why Iraq would not be a main aggressor against Israel. Yet, as we see today, Hussein has been pulled out of office, and Iraq (Babylon) will hold a different role in biblical prophecy, as in the book of Revelation.

After many days thou shalt be visited: in the latter years thou shalt come into the land that is brought back from the sword, that is gathered out of many peoples, upon the mountains of Israel, which have been a continual waste; but it is brought forth out of the peoples, and they shall dwell securely, all of them (Ezek. 38:8 ASV).

In verse 8, the phrase "after many days" is translated in Hebrew as "in the latter days" or "in the last days." The next phrase, "thou shalt come into the land," is referring to Israel being back in the land (which occurred on May 14, 1948, when Jews from all over the world returned to their land, fulfilling Ezekiel 37). Moving on, we read that the Jews "shall dwell securely." The word in Hebrew for "securely" is the beach, which means confidently; this implies that a peace treaty could be in place before this event.

> "And thou shalt ascend, thou shalt come like a storm, thou shalt be like a cloud to cover the land, thou, and all thy hordes, and many peoples with thee" (Ezek. 38:9 ASV). Many nations will come up against Israel and will cover the land. Thus saith the Lord Jehovah: It shall come to pass in that day, that things shall come into thy mind, and thou shalt devise an evil device: and thou shalt say, I will go up to the land of unwalled villages; I will go to them that are at rest, that dwell securely, all of them dwelling without walls, and having neither bars nor gates (Ezek. 38:10–11 ASV).

Again, "in that day," or better translated, "in the last days," these nations will come up with a plot to destroy Israel. It is interesting to consider the next verse about going up against a land of unwalled villages (or cities). This may not seem that strange in today's society; however, when this verse was written, all of the cities had gates and walls that protected them from enemies as well as protection for those who were leaving and entering the city. In today's society, our cities are unwalled.

"To take the spoil and to take the prey; to turn thy hand against the waste places that are [now] inhabited, and against the people that are gathered out of the nations, that have gotten cattle and goods, that dwell in the middle of the earth (Ezek. 38:12 ASV). This speaks of the nations moving in to take over the land and possessions of the inhabitants.

"Sheba, and Dedan, and the merchants of Tarshish, with all the young lions thereof, shall say unto thee, Art thou come to take the spoil? hast thou assembled thy company to take the prey? To carry away silver and gold, to take away cattle and goods, to take great spoil?" (Ezek. 38:13 ASV). Sheba and Dedan represent Saudi Arabia. It seems they are speaking up against the war (they could be taking a neutral position in fear of getting involved). They are not taking action, along with the young lions, who represent the united kingdom, who seem to voice their words yet take no physical action.

"Therefore, son of man, prophesy, and say unto Gog, Thus saith the Lord Jehovah: In that day when my people Israel dwelleth securely, shalt thou not know it?" (Ezek. 38:14 ASV). Again the Lord emphasizes that this event will take place in the latter days, when Israel is back in the land, dwelling securely.

And thou shalt come from thy place out of the uttermost parts of the north, thou, and many peoples with thee, all of them riding upon horses, a great company and a mighty army; and thou shalt come up against my people Israel, as a cloud to cover the land: it shall come to pass in the latter days, that I will bring thee against my land, that the nations may know me, when I shall be sanctified in thee, O Gog, before their eyes. Thus, saith the Lord Jehovah: Art thou he of whom I spake in old time by my servants the prophets of Israel, that prophesied in those days for [many] years that I would bring thee against them? And it shall come to pass in that day when Gog shall come against the land of Israel, saith the Lord Jehovah, that my wrath shall come up into my nostrils (Ezek. 38:15–18 ASV).

Once more, we are told that the nations north of Israel shall come against the Lord's people. The Lord will intervene, and His wrath will come against these nations. The Bible has depicted an angel wiping out an army of 10,000 Syrian men outside the walls of Jerusalem, as well as the Lord performing miracles by taking down the walls of Jericho. With God all things are possible (Matt. 19:26); because He is the creator of all things, there is nothing the Lord cannot do! The Lord goes on to say the nations of the world will know that He is God.

> *For in my jealousy and the fire of my wrath have I spoken, Surely in that day there shall be a great shaking in the land of Israel; so that the fishes of the sea, and the birds of the heavens, and the beasts of the field, and all creeping things that creep upon the earth, and all the men that are upon the face of the earth, shall shake at my presence, and the mountains shall be thrown down, and the steep places shall fall, and every wall shall fall to the ground (Ezek. 38:19–20 ASV).*

The Lord is referring to a great earthquake and to supernatural powers that will make His presence known. Interestingly, in Zechariah 12:1–19, God talks about making Jerusalem a burden to all who come against them and that He will destroy all nations that come up against Jerusalem.

"And I will call for a sword against him unto all my mountains, saith the Lord Jehovah: every man's sword shall be against his brother" (Ezek. 38:21 ASV). God reiterates that every man will be for himself. There will be so much confusion and so many catastrophic events taking place that men will fight against each other to survive. There are many situations throughout the Bible where nations set out to destroy Israel but ended up killing each other (such as when Gideon and his 300 men overcame their enemies by confusion).

> *And with pestilence and with blood will I enter into judgment with him; and I will rain upon him, and upon his hordes, and upon the many peoples that are with him, an overflowing shower, and great hailstones, fire, and brimstone. And I will magnify myself, and sanctify myself, and I will make myself known in the eyes of many nations, and they shall know that I am Jehovah (Ezek. 38:22–23).*

The Lord will make Himself known to Israel as He did in the days of Moses and Israel's deliverance from Egypt. The Lord will supernaturally intercede for His people, and they will know He is the Lord! After the Israelites crossed the Red Sea with Moses and were fed manna from the heavens, they quickly forgot about the miracles God performed. How many ways can the Lord make Himself known to the Jews? But still, they fail to embrace Him. The Bible says the Jews will accept the Antichrist as their messiah for a short time—that is until he shows his true nature by demanding to be worshipped in the temple he builds in Jerusalem.

As we enter into chapter 39 of Ezekiel, we get a recap of chapter 38 as well as some interesting insights into how to bury the dead and how Israel will come back to the Lord.

Ezekiel 39

> *And thou, son of man, prophesy against Gog and say, Thus saith the Lord Jehovah: Behold, I am against thee, O Gog, prince of Rosh, Meshech, and Tubal: and I will turn thee about, and will lead thee on, and will cause thee to come up from the uttermost parts of the north; and I will bring thee upon the mountains of Israel, and I will smite thy bow out of thy left hand, and will cause thine arrows to fall out of thy right hand. Thou shalt fall*

upon the mountains of Israel, thou, and all thy hordes, and the peoples that are with thee: I will give thee unto the ravenous birds of every sort, and to the beasts of the field to be devoured. Thou shalt fall upon the open field; for I have spoken it, saith the Lord Jehovah (Ezek. 39:1–5 ASV).

Here is a recap of prior verses in Ezekiel 38 with greater details of how the Lord will disarm the enemies. "And I will smite thy bow out of thy left hand, and will cause thine arrows to fall out of thy right hand" (Ezek. 39:3 ASV).

In the early century, from the land of Magog came the Scythians, who were best known for their archery skills. They were able to ride on a horse at full gallop and shoot a bird out of the sky. (With today's high-tech weapons, this does not require great skill.)

And I will send a fire on Magog, and them that dwell securely in the isles; and shall know that I am Jehovah. And my holy name will I make known amid my people Israel; neither will I suffer my holy name to be profaned anymore more creations shall know that I am Jehovah, the Holy One in Israel (Ezek. 39:6–7 ASV).

The Lord judged Sodom and Gomorrah with fire and brimstone; here He will do it again. Genesis 1:1 states that in the beginning, God created the heavens and the earth. Therefore, with Him all things are possible! When the Lord says He will do something, we can be assured that it will happen!

Behold, it cometh, and it shall be done, saith the Lord Jehovah; this is the day whereof I have spoken. And they that dwell in the cities of Israel shall go forth, and shall make fires of the weapons and burn them, both the shields and the bucklers, the bows and the arrows, and the hand staves, and the spears, and they shall make fires of them seven years; so that they shall take no wood out of the field, neither cut down any out of the forests; for they shall make fires of the weapons; and they shall plunder those that plundered them, and rob those that robbed them, saith the Lord Jehovah (Ezek. 39:8–10 ASV).

Israel will be able to use the plundered weapons as fuel for seven years. (Isn't it interesting that the shelf life of a nuclear warhead is also seven years?)

And it shall come to pass in that day, that I will give unto Gog a place for burial in Israel, the valley of them that pass through on the east of the sea; and it shall stop them that pass through: and there shall they bury Gog and all his multitude; and they shall call it The valley of Hamongog. And seven months shall the house of Israel be burying them, that they may cleanse the land. Yea, all the people of the land shall bury them; and it shall be to them a renown in the day that I shall be glorified, saith the Lord Jehovah. And they shall set apart men of continual employment, that shall pass through the land, and, with them that pass through, those that bury them that remain upon the face of the land, to cleanse it: after the end of seven months shall they search. And they that pass through the land shall pass through; and when any seeth a man's bone, then shall he set up a sign by it, till the buriers have buried it in the valley of Hamon-Gog. And Hamonah shall also be the name of a city. Thus shall they cleanse the land (Ezek. 39:11–16 ASV).

The Lord has already planned a burial place east of the Dead Sea for Gog and his armies. Professionals will be hired to bury the dead. If a civilian sees any bones, he is to not touch them but to put up a flag to mark the spot so the professional gravedigger can dispose of them. We could not have imagined what this verse was referring to before the 1940s. Today, we do understand the effects of nuclear, biological, and chemical warfare.

Zechariah 14:12 also describes the nuclear effects that will occur in the last days:

> *And this shall be the plague with which the LORD will strike all the people who fought against Jerusalem: Their flesh shall dissolve while they stand on their feet, Their eyes shall dissolve in their sockets, And their tongues shall dissolve in their mouths (NKJV).*

The Lord said in Daniel 12:4 to seal up the book until the end when knowledge will be increased. Could we be living in the last days? Is this what God was speaking of when He told Daniel that knowledge would increase and then we would understand the meaning of His words? The Lord foretold all of these events thousands of years ago, and now these verses are making sense. Just think about our forefathers, these godly men, and women who read the Bible 200-plus years ago and came across verses like this. It must have been hard for them to understand, but they fervently trusted in the Lord anyway. We are living in times when the Bible's predictions make complete sense to us; yet many people refuse to heed the words of our Lord.

Yes! God predicted the past, present, and future. All we have to do is accept His invitation and abide in Him, and we will be saved. For God sent His only Son to die on the cross; then in three days, He arose from the grave so that we can have everlasting life. Incredible—the God of this universe made Himself a man to experience the suffering of the flesh. He took our sins and crucified them forever on the cross.

> *And thou, son of man, thus saith the Lord Jehovah: Speak unto the birds of every sort, and to every beast of the field, Assemble yourselves, and come; gather yourselves on every side to my sacrifice that I do*

> *sacrifice for you, even a great sacrifice upon the mountains of Israel, that ye may eat flesh and drink blood. Ye shall eat the flesh of the mighty, and drink the blood of the princes of the earth, of rams, of lambs, and of goats, of bullocks, all of them fatlings of Bashan. And ye shall eat fat till ye be full, and drink blood till ye be drunken, of my sacrifice which I have sacrificed for you. And ye shall be filled at my table with horses and chariots, with mighty men, and with all men of war, saith the Lord Jehovah (Ezek. 39:17–20 ASV).*

From verse 17 on, we move into the latter part of the seven years. These verses pick up with the Battle of Armageddon, where the birds of the earth will feast on the flesh of those dead in the Valley of Megiddo.

"And I will set my glory among the nations, and all the nations shall see my judgment that I have executed, and my hand that I have laid upon them. So the house of Israel shall know that I am Jehovah their God, from that day and forward (Ezek. 39:21–22 ASV). This is referring to Revelation 19 when Christ returns with His church and wipes out the armies of the world. At last, the house of Israel will know that He is the Lord. He will set His right foot on the Mount of Olives and split the mount in two.

> *And the nations shall know that the house of Israel went into captivity for their iniquity; because they trespassed against me, and I hid my face from them: so I gave them into the hand of their adversaries, and they fell all of them by the sword. According to their uncleanness and according to their transgressions did I unto them, and I hid my face from them. Therefore thus saith the Lord Jehovah: Now will I bring back the captivity of Jacob, and have mercy upon the whole house of Israel; and I will be jealous for my holy name. And they shall bear their shame, and all their trespasses whereby*

they have trespassed against me when they shall dwell securely in their land, and none shall make them afraid (Ezek. 39:23–26 ASV).

When I have brought them back from the peoples, and gathered them out of their enemies lands, and am sanctified in them in the sight of many nations. And they shall know that I am Jehovah their God, in that I caused them to go into captivity among the nations, and have gathered them unto their land; and I will leave none of them any more there; neither will I hide my face any more from them; for I have poured out my Spirit upon the house of Israel, saith the Lord Jehovah (Ezek. 39:27–29 ASV).

The Lord said that He will pour out His Spirit again upon the house of Israel in the latter days. Romans 11:25 relates how the Holy Spirit is dealing with the Gentiles, and when the Lord has gathered His church (the fullness of the Gentiles) Christ will pour out His Spirit upon the nation of Israel again. Blindness has been put on the Jews (in part) until the fullness of the Gentiles is achieved. God is not done with the nation of Israel, but He is pouring out His Spirit upon His Church. Once the Lord takes His Church (in the Rapture), He will make Himself known to the Jews who have rejected Him. So the question arises: When will this event take place?

We don't know the day or time, only the season! Our Lord has said, "Now when these things begin to happen, look up and lift your heads, because your redemption draws near" (Luke 21:28 NKJV). Israel is God's prophetic time clock for the Last Days. As of now, we are in between Ezekiel 37 and 38. Ezekiel 37 puts Israel back in the land (May 14, 1948), and Ezekiel 40 speaks of the rebuilding of the temple. The battle that occurs in Ezekiel 38 must take place either right after the Church is removed (the Rapture) or within weeks of it, if not simultaneously. Though we can only speculate on when this event will take place, the Bible does support two key verses that put this event in the last seven-year period. Both Daniel and Ezekiel allude to these seven years. Keep in mind what Jesus preached in Luke 4:18–21:

> *"The Spirit of the LORD is upon Me Because He has anointed Me To preach the gospel to the poor; He has sent Me to heal the broken hearted, To proclaim liberty to the captives And recovery of sight to the blind, To set at liberty those who are oppressed; To proclaim the acceptable year of the LORD." Then He closed the book and gave it back to the attendant and sat down. And the eyes of all who were in the synagogue were fixed on Him. And He began to say to them, "Today this Scripture is fulfilled in your hearing."*

Jesus did not go on to read the rest of the verse in Isaiah 61:2: "And the day of vengeance of our God; To comfort all who mourn." Christ put a period where there is a question mark. He stated that the Scripture was fulfilled, but He did not read about the vengeance of God, which again leads us back to the last seven years of world history when God shall pour out His wrath and vengeance on a sinful world that has rejected Him. God has preserved His Word for thousands of years. He has laid out in advance the details of world history. He foretold our past, present, and future. His Word has proven to be 100 percent accurate thus far. It is important to take a close look at what God is saying to us. Step back into the late nineteenth century. Try grasping these verses in the Bible. It would seem like nonsense or science fiction to read about countries being wiped out in one hour, a cashless society, professional gravediggers clearing dead bodies due to nuclear contamination, or the verses in Zechariah that speak of tongues dissolving in mouths and eyes being dissolved in their sockets. Do you see how farfetched this would have sounded a hundred years or more ago?

However, in the twenty-first century (since knowledge has increased), these are the technologies we read about daily in medical journals and military reports. Yes, the Lord has spoken it. And yes, it will come to pass. Blessed be the name of the Lord!

Chapter 9:
Mene, Mene, Tekel Upharsin

An Overview of the Book of Daniel

Imagine predicting the future! What would it be like to receive a vision, write it down, and then, hundreds or even thousands of years later, have these predictions come true? The book of Daniel does this. Daniel, a man of God, purposed in his heart to serve the Lord, and God was faithful and blessed Daniel. God revealed visions to Daniel that laid out world history, including "end time" scenarios. This prophetic book is the key to understanding Bible prophecy—Old Testament writings that foretell the future. Let's look at a synopsis of the book of Daniel to better understand God's divine plan.

The Book of Daniel was written between the years 605 and 570 BC, in both Hebrew and Chaldeans (it also included a few Persian words). Interestingly, Christ quoted from Daniel three times in the New Testament. Also, keep in mind that Daniel is the only book in the Bible that has a chapter (4) written by a Gentile king (King Nebuchadnezzar), declaring the signs and wonders of the highest God and the greatness of His works. As we read on, we notice that God used Nebuchadnezzar to punish the Jews for their disobedience, as stated in verse 2 of chapter 1: "The Lord gave Jehoiakim king of Judah into [Nebuchadnezzar's] hand."

We then discover that this upright man, Daniel, was blessed by God and shown favor. Daniel was appointed by God to reveal dreams and to receive visions so we may have insight into God's plan for His people; the nations of the world; and us, the saints of His church who are established through our Lord and Savior Jesus Christ.

The book of Daniel can be broken down into two sections. Chapters 1 to 6 are narrative and historic, while chapters 7 to 12 are more about visions and dreams. Chapters 1 through 2:3 and chapters 8 through 12 were written in Hebrew (the language of the Jews), whereas chapters 2:4–7 were written in Chaldean (the language of the Gentiles). This is important to point out because we can distinguish what God promised to the Jewish nation. Also, we will learn as we study the book of Daniel that there are visions that parallel the book of Revelation—Daniel and the apostle John saw the same visions. It's time to begin the studies of what God wants to reveal to us. Warning! These events have been or will be fulfilled as prophesied.

Daniel Chapter 1

In chapter 1 the Lord gave Jerusalem into the hands of Nebuchadnezzar, and the vessels of the temple were carried off to Babylon. You might ask yourself, why would the Lord give His people into the hands of a Gentile king? The answer lies in Leviticus 25, where the Lord told Moses there was to be a Sabbath year of rest for the land every seven years. After every six years of sowing, pruning, and harvesting, the fields were to be left unsowed and the vineyards unpruned during the seventh year. The Israelites did not obey God in this. Therefore, He punished them for seventy years, leading them into captivity and giving the land seventy years of rest.

Reading on in Daniel, we discover that King Nebuchadnezzar instructed Ashpenaz (the head eunuch) to choose young men who were gifted with wisdom to study and serve in the king's court. Daniel and three of his friends were among those chosen for this task. We then notice that Daniel and his friends stayed dedicated to the Lord, and the Lord blessed them and exalted them to high positions within the king's court.

> *In the third year of the reign of Jehoiakim king of Judah came Nebuchadnezzar king of Babylon unto Jerusalem, and besieged it. And the Lord gave Jehoiakim king of Judah into his hand, with part of the vessels of the house of God: which he carried into the land of Shinar to the house of his god; and he brought the vessels into the treasure house of his god. And the king spake unto Ashpenaz the master of his eunuchs, that he should bring certain of the children of Israel, and of the king's seed, and the princes; Children in whom was no blemish, but well favored, and skillful in all wisdom, and cunning in knowledge, and understanding science, and such as had ability in them to stand in the king's palace, and whom they might teach the learning and the tongue of the Chaldeans. And the king appointed them a daily provision of the king's meat, and of the wine which he drank: so nourishing them three years, that at the end thereof they might stand before the king. Now among these were of the children of Judah, Daniel, Hananiah, Mishael, and Azariah: Unto whom the prince of the eunuchs gave names: for he gave unto Daniel the name of Belteshazzar; and to Hananiah, of Shadrach; and Mishael, of Meshach; and to Azariah, of Abednego. But Daniel purposed in his heart that he would not defile himself with the portion of the king's meat, nor with the wine which he drank: therefore he requested of the prince of the eunuchs*

that he might not defile himself. Now God had brought
Daniel into favor and tender love with the prince of the
eunuchs. And the prince of the eunuchs said unto Daniel, I fear
my lord the king, who hath appointed your meat and your
drink: for why should he see your faces worse liking than the
children which are of your sort? then shall ye make me
endanger my head to the king. Then said Daniel to Melzar,
whom the prince of the eunuchs had set over Daniel,
Hananiah, Mishael, and Azariah, Prove thy servants, I beseech
thee, ten days; and let them give us pulse to eat, and water to
drink. Then let our countenances be looked upon before thee,
and the countenance of the children that eat of the portion of
the king's meat: and as thou seest, deal with thy servants. So
he consented to them in this matter and proved them ten days.
And at the end of ten days, their countenances appeared fairer
and fatter in flesh than all the children who did eat the portion
of the king's meat. Thus Melzar took away the portion of their
meat, and the wine that they should drink; and gave them
pulse. As for these four children, God gave them knowledge
and skill in all learning and wisdom: and Daniel had
understanding in all visions and dreams. Now at the end of the
days that the king had said he should bring them in, then the
prince of the eunuchs brought them in before
Nebuchadnezzar. And the king communed with them; and
among them, all was found none like Daniel, Hananiah,
Mishael, and Azariah: therefore good they before the king. And
in all matters of wisdom and understanding that the king
enquired of them he found them ten times better than all the
magicians and astrologers that were in all his realm. And
Daniel continued even unto the first year of King Cyrus (Dan.
1).

Daniel Chapter 2

This chapter reports a very strange dream that King
Nebuchadnezzar had. He then insists the chief magicians, the
astrologers, and the sorcerers reveal his dream to him,

without ever revealing to them any knowledge of what the dream was. (Perhaps Nebuchadnezzar wanted to see if these hired hands were worth their salaries.) Nebuchadnezzar was a general of the Babylonian army; his father died during the siege of Jerusalem, and Nebechadnezzer inherited the throne. Therefore he also inherited the staff who had been appointed by his father. The Scriptures state that these men were unable to reveal the dream to the king.

Now comes a powerful demonstration of how our God displays His always-perfect plans. "For as the heavens are higher than the earth, so are My ways higher than your ways" Isaiah 55:9. Romans 8:28 reminds us that "All things work together for good to those who love God, to those who are the called according to His purpose"(NKJV).

Because God's chosen people had disobeyed Him, He allowed them to be captured and led away. Now Daniel was in the right place at the right time to be used by God. He was being called by God to be an ambassador to Nebuchadnezzar. When none of the court appointees were able to interpret the dream, Daniel sent a message to the king. When he was before the king Daniel stated the God of heaven could reveal the dream and its interpretation to him. As we read on, we see Daniel seeking the Lord in prayer and the Lord giving Daniel the dream with its interpretation.

> *And in the second year of the reign of Nebuchadnezzar, he dreamed dreams, wherewith his spirit was troubled, and his sleep broke from him. Then the king commanded to call the magicians, the astrologers, the sorcerers, and the Chaldeans, to shew the king his dreams. So they came and stood before the king. And the king said unto them, I have dreamed a dream, and my spirit was troubled to know the dream. Then spake the Chaldeans to the king in Syriac king, live forever: tell thy servants the dream, and we will shew*

the interpretation. The king answered and said to the Chaldeans, The thing is gone from me: if ye will not make known unto me the dream, with the interpretation thereof, ye shall be cut in pieces, and your houses shall be made a dunghill. But if ye shew the dream, and the interpretation thereof, ye shall receive of me gifts and rewards and great honor, therefore, shew me the dream and the interpretation thereof. They answered again and said, Let the king tell his servants the dream, and we will shew the interpretation of it. The king answered and said, I know of certainty that ye would gain the tie because ye see the thing is gone from me. But if ye will not make known unto me the dream, there is but one decree for you: for ye have prepared to lie and corrupt words to speak before me, till the time be changed: therefore tell me the dream, and I shall know that ye can shew me the interpretation thereof. The Chaldeans answered before the king, and said, There is not a man upon the earth that can shew the king's matter: therefore there is no king, lord, nor ruler, that asked such things at any magician, or astrologer, or Chaldean. And it is a rare thing that the king requireth and there is none other that can shew it before the king, except the gods, whose dwelling is not with flesh. For this cause, the king was angry and commanded to destroy all the wise men of Babylon. And the decree went forth that the wise men should be slain, and they sought Daniel and his fellows to be slain. Then Daniel answered with counsel and wisdom to Arioch the captain of the king's guard, which was gone forth to slay the wise men of Babylon: He answered and said to Arioch the king's captain, Why is the decree so hasty from the king? Then Arioch made the thing known to Daniel. Then Daniel went in and desired of the king that he would give him time, and that he would shew the king the interpretation. Then Daniel went to his house and made the thing known to

Hananiah, Mishael, and Azariah, his companions: That they would desire mercies of the God of heaven concerning this secret; that Daniel and his fellows should not perish with the rest of the wise men of Babylon. Then was the secret revealed unto Daniel in a night vision. Then Daniel blessed the God of heaven. Daniel answered and said, Blessed be the name of God forever and ever: for wisdom and might are his: And he changeth the times and the seasons: he removeth kings, and setteth up kings: he giveth wisdom unto the wise, and knowledge to them that know to understand: He revealeth the deep and secret things: he knoweth what is in the darkness, and the light dwelleth with him. I thank thee and praise thee, O thou God of my fathers, who hast given me wisdom and might, and hast made known unto me now what we desired of thee: for thou hast now made known unto us the king's matter. Therefore Daniel went in unto Arioch, whom the king had ordained to destroy the wise men of Babylon: he went and said thus unto him; Destroy not the wise men of Babylon: bring me in before the king, and I will shew unto the king the interpretation. Then Arioch brought in Daniel before the king in haste and said thus unto him, I have found a man of the captives of Judah, that will make known unto the king the interpretation. The king answered and said to Daniel, whose name was Belteshazzar, Art thou able to make known unto me the dream which I have seen, and the interpretation thereof? Daniel answered in the presence of the king, and said, The secret which the king hath demanded cannot the wise men, the astrologers, the magicians, the soothsayers, shew unto the king; But there is a God in heaven that revealeth secrets, and maketh known to the king Nebuchadnezzar what shall be in the latter days. Thy dream, and the visions of thy head upon thy bed, are these; As for thee, O king, thy thoughts came into thy mind upon thy bed, what should come to pass hereafter: and he that revealeth secrets maketh known to thee what shall come to pass. But as for me, this secret is not revealed to me for any wisdom that I have more than any living, but for their sakes that shall make known the interpretation to the king, and that thou mightiest know the thoughts of thy heart. Thou, O king, sawest, and behold a great image. This great image, whose brightness was excellent, stood before thee; and the form thereof was terrible. This image's head was of fine gold, his breast and his arms of silver, his belly and his thighs of brass, His legs of iron, his feet part of iron and part of clay. Thou sawest till that a stone was cut out without hands, which smote the image upon his feet that were of iron and clay, and brake them to pieces. Then was the iron, the clay, the brass, the silver, and the gold, broken to pieces together, and became like the chaff of the summer threshing floors; and the wind carried them away, that no place was found for them: and the stone that smote the image became a great mountain, and filled the whole earth. This is the dream, and we will tell the interpretation thereof before the king. Thou, O king, art a king of kings: for the God of heaven hath given thee a kingdom, power, strength, and glory. And wheresoever the children of men dwell, the beasts of the field and the fowls of the heaven hath he given into thine hand and hath made thee ruler over them all. Thou art this head of gold. And after thee shall arise another kingdom inferior to thee, and another third kingdom of brass, which shall bear rule over all the earth. And the fourth kingdom shall be strong as iron: forasmuch as iron breaketh in pieces and subdueth all things: and as iron that breaketh all these, shall it break in pieces and bruise. And whereas thou sawest the feet and toes, part of potters' clay, and part of iron, the kingdom shall be divided; but there shall be in it of the strength of the iron, forasmuch as thou sawest the iron mixed with miry clay. And as the toes of the feet were part of iron, and part of clay, so the kingdom shall be partly strong, and partly broken. And whereas thou sawest iron mixed with miry clay, they shall mingle themselves with the seed of men: but they shall not cleave one to another, even as iron is not mixed with clay. And in the days of these kings shall the God of heaven set up a kingdom, which shall never be destroyed: and the kingdom shall not be left to other people, but it shall break in pieces and consume all these kingdoms, and it shall stand forever. Forasmuch as thou sawest that the stone was cut out of the mountain without hands and that it brake in pieces the iron, the brass, the clay, the silver, and the gold; the great God hath made known to the king what shall come to pass hereafter: and the dream is certain, and the interpretation thereof sure. Then the king Nebuchadnezzar fell upon his face and worshipped Daniel, and commanded that they should offer an oblation and sweet odors unto him. The king answered unto Daniel, and said, Of a truth it is, that your God is a God of gods, and a Lord of kings, and a revealer of secrets, seeing thou couldest reveal this secret. Then the king made Daniel a great man and gave him many great gifts, and made him ruler over the whole province of Babylon, and chief of the governors over all the wise men of Babylon. Then Daniel requested the king, and he set Shadrach, Meshach, and Abednego, over the affairs of the province of Babylon: but Daniel sat in the gate of the king (Dan. 2).

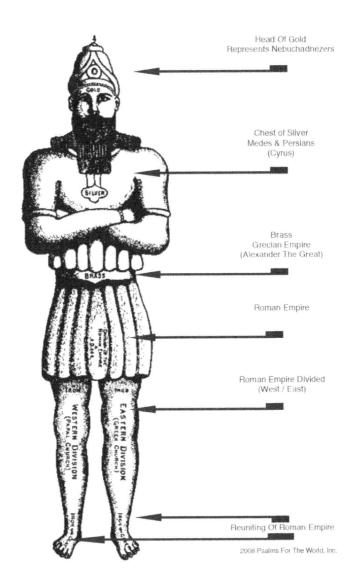

Head Of Gold
Represents Nebuchadnezers

Chest of Silver
Medes & Persians
(Cyrus)

Brass
Grecian Empire
(Alexander The Great)

Roman Empire

Roman Empire Divided
(West / East)

Reuniting Of Roman Empire

2008 Psalms For The World, Inc.

Interpretation of the Dream

Daniel, in verses 37 to 45, gives the interpretation of the dream. From world history, we can define these world empires as follows:

1. The head of gold represents Babylon
2. Chest and arms of silver represent Mede and Persia
3. The belly and thighs of bronze represent the Grecian Empire
4. Legs of iron, feet part iron, and part clay represent the Roman Empire
5. The stone that struck the image and broke it into pieces represents the kingdom of Jesus Christ (yet to come to pass)

History reveals to us that Cyrus (the Medes and Persians) conquered Babylon, followed by Alexander the Great (the Grecian Empire) and then Julius Caesar (the Roman Empire). In verses 40 to 44, we read of this fourth kingdom reuniting, stronger and weaker nations (iron and clay) coming together and becoming one. We must keep in mind that the Roman Empire was never conquered; it fell apart within (divided by Diocletian in AD 284, represented by the two legs of iron). Today's Roman Empire would be what we in the twenty-first century refer to as the European Union or the European Community, where stronger and weaker nations came together and became one.

Now let's reflect on World War II and what Nazi Germany did to Europe. Who would have ever thought that the Berlin Wall would come down and that these countries in Europe would reunite and become one, in addition to giving up the sovereignty of their currency and entering into a one-state economic system using the euro?

Now we can see in hindsight how Daniel's prophecies have been fulfilled with the first four empires. It is also interesting to note that commentaries on Daniel dating back to the nineteenth century predicted the rise of the fourth empire (Roman Empire), and these commentaries were written before the world wars. Let's also keep in mind that in museums today we can find manuscripts of the Septuagint, the

Hebrew Bible that was translated into Greek between 285 and 270 BC before the Roman Empire conquest), which again shows the authenticity of the Book of Daniel.

Daniel Chapter 3

Nebuchadnezzar decided (despite the dream that Daniel interpreted) that his kingdom would last forever. Therefore the king had a statue built of gold and commanded all to bow down and worship this image. This parallels Revelation 13:15, where an image was made and all men were forced to worship the image of the beast. In both Daniel and Revelation, those who did not bow down were sentenced to death.

Nebuchadnezzar the king made an image of gold, whose height was threescore cubits, and the breadth thereof six cubits: he set it up in the plain of Dura, in the province of Babylon. Then Nebuchadnezzar the king sent to gather together the princes, the governors, the captains, the judges, the treasurers, the counselors, the sheriffs, and all the rulers of the provinces, to come to the dedication of the image which Nebuchadnezzar the king had set up. Then the princes, the governors, captains, the judges, the treasurers, the counselor sheriffs, and all the rulers of the provinces, were gathered together unto the dedication of the image that Nebuchadnezzar the king had set up; and they stood before the image that Nebuchadnezzar had set up. Then a herald loudly proclaimed, "To you, it is commanded, O people, nations, and languages, that at what time ye hear the sound of the cornet, flute, harp, sackbut, psaltery, dulcimer, and all kinds of musick, ye fall and worship the golden image that King Nebuchadnezzar the king hath set up: And whoso falleth not down and worshippeth shall the same hour be cast into the midst of a burning fiery furnace. Therefore at that time, when all the people heard the sound of the cornet, flute, harp, sackbut, psaltery, and all kinds of music, all the people, the nations, and the languages, fell and worshipped the golden image that Nebuchadnezzar the king had set up. Wherefore at that time certain Chaldeans came near and accused the Jews. They spoke and said to King Nebuchadnezzar, "O king, live forever! Thou, O king, hast made a decree, that every man that shall hear the sound of the cornet, flute, harp, sackbut, psaltery, and dulcimer, and all kinds of music, shall fall and worship the golden image. And whoso falleth not down and worshippeth, that he should be cast into the midst of a burning fiery furnace. There are certain Jews whom thou hast set over the affairs of the province of Babylon, Shadrach, Meshach, and Abednego; these men, O king, have not regarded thee: they serve not thy gods, nor worship the golden image which thou hast set up. Then Nebuchadnezzar, in his rage and fury, commanded to bring Shadrach, Meshach, and Abednego. Then they brought these men before the king. Nebuchadnezzar spake and said unto them, Is it true, O Shadrach, Meshach, and Abednego, do not ye serve my gods, nor worship the golden image which I have set up? Now if ye be ready that at what time ye hear the sound of the cornet, flute, harp, sackbut, psaltery, and dulcimer, and all kinds of musick, ye fall and worship the image which I have made; well: but if ye worship not, ye shall be cast the same hour into the midst of a burning fiery furnace; and who is that God that shall deliver you out of my hands? Shadrach, Meshach, and Abednego answered and said to the king, "O Nebuchadnezzar, we are not careful to answer thee in this matter. If it is so, our God whom we serve can deliver us from the burning fiery furnace, and He will deliver us out of thine hand, O king. But if not, be it known unto thee, O king, that we will not serve thy gods nor worship the golden image which thou hast set up. Then Nebuchadnezzar became full of fury, and the form of his visage was changed against Shadrach, Meshach, and Abednego. Therefore, he spake, and commanded that they should heat the furnace one seven times more than it was wont to be heated. And he commanded the mightiest men that were in his army to bind Shadrach, Meshach, and Abednego, and to cast them into the burning fiery furnace. Then these men were bound in their coats, their hosen, their hats, and their other garments, and were cast into the midst of the burning fiery furnace. Therefore, because the king's commandment was urgent, and the furnace exceeding hot, the flames of the fire slew those men that took up Shadrach, Meshach, and Abednego. And these three men, Shadrach, Meshach, and Abednego, fell into the midst of the burning fiery furnace. Then Nebuchadnezzar the king was astonished, and rose in haste, and spoke, and said unto his counselors not we cast three men bound into the midst of the fire? They answered and said unto the king, True, O king. He answered and said, Look, I see four men loose king in the mid-fire, and they have no hurt, and the fourth is like the Son of God. Then Nebuchadnezzar came near to the mouth of the burning fiery furnace, and spake, and said, Shadrach, Meshach, and Abednego, ye servants of the highest God, come forth, and come hither. Then Shadrach, Meshach, and Abednego came forth amid the fire. And the princes, governors, and captains, and the king's counselors being gathered together, saw these men, upon whose bodies the fire had no power, nor was a hair of their head singed, neither were their coats changed, nor the smell of fire had passed on them. Then Nebuchadnezzar spake, and said, Blessed be the God of Shadrach, Meshach, and Abednego, who hath sent his angel, and delivered his servants that trusted in him, and have changed the king's word, and yielded their bodies, that they might not serve nor worship any god, except their own God. Therefore I make a decree, That every people, nation, and language, which speak thing amiss against the God of Shadrach, Meshach, and Abednego, shall be cut in pieces, and their houses shall be made a dunghill: because there is no other God that can deliver after this sort. Then the king promoted Shadrach, Meshach, and Abednego in the province of Babylon (Dan. 3).

The king erected an image representing his kingdom to reign forever. We then notice that those who did not bow and worship the image were sentenced to death. Three Hebrew men did not bow down and worship when they heard the instruments, and so they were sentenced to be cast into a fiery furnace. Nebuchadnezzar commanded that the furnace be heated up seven times hotter; it was so hot that the soldiers who threw the Hebrew men in were burnt to death. (According to Chuck Missler in his Expositional Commentary on Daniel, today's archeologists have located these ancient days in modern-day Iraq.)

These three men were walking in the fiery furnace, and a fourth one, "like the Son of God" was with them. Keep in consideration that the Old Testament is Christ concealed and the New Testament is Christ revealed. Then this would be a picture of Christ going through the fiery furnace with His people. This is a perfect example of the Rapture of the church and the 144,000 Jews that go through the tribulation period protected by God (Rev. 7:4). To illustrate this better, let's take a closer look at the text of Daniel chapter 3.

To start, we should be aware of what is not said in the text. It describes three Hebrew men, with no mention of Daniel. It is the book he wrote, yet he is not mentioned in this chapter. Later in chapter 6, when the decree has gone out that all are commanded to worship the king, Daniel remained faithful to

God and continued with his daily prayers. His punishment for his disobedience was being thrown into the lions' den. So the question is, in chapter 3, where was Daniel? Although the text does not say, some scholars believe that since Daniel was in charge of the king's affairs, he may have been out of the country on the king's behalf. Perhaps the Holy Spirit left Daniel out of this chapter to illustrate that Daniel was a type of the Church, which is pulled out or raptured before the great tribulation, as seen in Revelation 3:10. The other three Hebrew men may represent the 144,000 Jews who are sealed or protected by God during the great tribulation, as described in Revelation 7:4.

In the book of Genesis, we see a similar illustration. Noah and his family went through the flood (protected by God), while Enoch, who preceded Noah, was taken out, or raptured. "And Enoch walked with God: and he was not; for God took him" (Gen. 5:24).

In Daniel 3:28, the king praised the God of Shadrach, Meshach, and Abednego, who sent His angel and delivered them from the fiery furnace. The king promoted these three Hebrew men and acknowledged the power of their God. Again notice how there are no mistakes with God and His plan. All things do work together for good.

Daniel Chapter 4

In chapter 4, King Nebuchadnezzar wrote a letter to the whole world, "unto all people, nations, and languages, that dwell in all the earth," and the king declared the signs and wonders of our Lord. (Take special note: This is the only chapter in the Bible that was written by a Gentile king.) How interesting that King Nebuchadnezzar gives praise to God and acknowledges His power, might, and dominion over all things. The king then gives a recap of the dream he had, as well as Daniel's interpretation given by God.

Mene, Mene, Tekel Upharsin

Nebuchadnezzar the king, unto all people, nations, and languages, that dwell in all the earth; Peace be multiplied unto you. thought it good to shew the signs and wonders that the high God hath wrought toward me. How great are his signs! and how mighty are his wonders! His kingdom is an everlasting kingdom, and his dominion is from generation to generation. I Nebuchadnezzar was at rest in mine house, and flourishing in my palace: saw a dream which made me afraid, and the thoughts upon my bed and the visions of my head troubled me. Therefore made I a decree to bring in all the wise men of Babylon before me, that they might make known unto me the interpretation of the dream. Then came in the magicians, the astrologers, the Chaldeans, and the soothsayers: and I told the dream before them; but they did not make known unto me the interpretation thereof. But at the last Daniel came in before me, whose name was Belteshazzar, according to the name of my God, and in whom is the spirit of the holy gods: and before him I told the dream, saying, O Belteshazzar, master of the magicians because I know that the spirit of the holy gods is in thee, and no secret troubleth thee, tell me the visions of my dream that I have seen, and the interpretation thereof. Thus were the visions of mine head in my bed; I saw, and behold a tree amid the earth, and the height thereof was great. The tree grew and was strong, and the height thereof reached unto heaven, and the sight thereof to the end of all the earth: The leaves thereof were fair, and the fruit thereof much, and in it was meat for all: the beasts of the field had shadow under it, and the fowls of the heaven dwelt in the boughs thereof, and all flesh was fed of it. I saw in the visions of my head upon my bed, and, behold, a watcher and a holy one came down from heaven; He cried aloud, and said thus, Hew down the tree, and cut off his branches, shake off his leaves, and scatter his fruit: let the beasts get away from under it, and the fowls from his branches: Nevertheless leave the stump of his roots in the earth, even with a band of iron and brass, in the tender grass of the field; and let it be wet with the dew of heaven, and let his portion be with the beasts in the grass of the earth: Let his heart be changed from man's, and let a beast's heart be given unto him, and let seven times pass over him. This matter is by the decree of the watchers, and the demand by the word of the holy ones: to the intent that the living may know that the highest ruleth in the kingdom of men, and giveth it to whomsoever he will, and setteth up over it the basest of men. This dream I King Nebuchadnezzar have seen. Now thou, O Belteshazzar, declare the interpretation thereof, forasmuch as all the wise men of my kingdom are not able to make known unto me the interpretation: but thou art able; for the spirit of the holy gods is in thee. Then Daniel, whose name was Belteshazzar, was astonied for one hour, and his thoughts troubled him. The king spake, and said, Belteshazzar, let not the dream, or the interpretation thereof, trouble thee. Belteshazzar answered and said, My lord, the dream be to them that hate thee, and the interpretation thereof to thine enemies. The tree that thou sawest, which grew, and was strong, whose height reached unto the heaven, and the sight thereof to all the earth; Whose leaves were fair, and the fruit thereof much, and in it was meat for all; under which the beasts of the field dwelt, and upon whose branches the fowls of the heaven had their habitation: It is thou, O king, that art grew and become strong: for thy greatness is grown, and reacheth unto heaven, and thy dominion to the end of the earth. And whereas the king saw a watcher and a holy one coming down from heaven, and saying, Hew the tree down, and destroy it; yet leave the stump of the roots thereof in the earth, even with a band of iron and brass, in the tender grass of the field; and let it be wet with the dew of heaven, and let his portion be with the beasts of the field, till seven times pass over him; This is the interpretation, O king, and this is the decree of the highest which is come upon my lord the king: That they shall drive thee from men, and thy dwelling shall be with the beasts of the field, and they shall make thee eat grass as oxen, and they shall wet thee with the dew of heaven, and seven times shall pass over thee, till thou know that the highest in the kingdom of men, and giveth it to whomsoever he will. And whereas they commanded to leave the stump of the tree roots; thy kingdom shall be sure unto thee, after that thou shalt have known that the heavens do rule. Wherefore, O king, let my counsel be acceptable unto thee and break off thy sins by righteousness, and thine iniquities by shew are showing to the poor; if it may be a lengthening of thy tranquillity. All this came upon the king Nebuchadnezzar. At the end of twelve months, he walked into the palace of the kingdom of Babylon. The king spake, and said, Is not this great Babylon, that I have built for the house of the kingdom by the might of my power, and for the honor of my majesty? While the word was in the king's mouth, there fell a voice from heaven, saying, O king Nebuchadnezzar, to thee it is spoken; The kingdom is departed from thee. And they shall drive thee from men, and thy dwelling shall be with the beasts of the field: they shall make thee to eat grass as oxen, and seven times shall pass over the until thou know that the highest ruleth in the kingdom of men, and giveth it to whomsoever he will. The same hour was the thing fulfilled upon Nebuchadnezzar: and he was driven from men, and did eat grass as oxen, and his body was wet with the dew of heaven, till his hairs were grown like eagles' feathers, and his nails like birds' claws. And at the end of the days, Nebuchadnezzar lifted mine eyes unto heaven, and mine understanding returned unto me, and I blessed the highest, and I praised and honored him that liveth forever, whose dominion is an everlasting dominion, and his kingdom is from generation to generation: And all the inhabitants of the earth are reputed as nothing: and he doeth according to his will in the army of heaven, and among the inhabitants of the earth: and none can stay his hand, or say unto him, What doest thou? At the same time, my reason returned unto me; and for the glory of my kingdom, dishonored brightness returned unto me; and my counselors and my lords sought unto me, and was established in my kingdom, and excellent majesty was added unto me. Now I Nebuchadnezzar praise and extol and honoree King of heaven, all whose works are truth, and his ways judgment: and those that walk in pride he is the case (Dan. 4).

King Nebuchadnezzar called upon Daniel to interpret his dream. In verse 8, the king called Daniel by his Hebrew name. This would imply that Daniel and the king had a close relationship; the text would support a personal bond between these two men. We then notice in verse 19 that Daniel was troubled; in fact, he felt compassion for the king, as he wished that the events in the dream might come upon the king's enemies and those who hated him. Another interesting fact about the book of Daniel is that, like in the book of Revelation, Daniel always gives the reader an interpretation of visions or dreams. As we read on, we discover the king had received a message from God. Nebuchadnezzar was caught up in his pride and became arrogant, bragging about his great city and kingdom. God hates pride and therefore had to strip Nebuchadnezzar of his kingdom (for seven years) until the king could humble himself and revere the true and living God.

The text relates that within an hour, Nebuchadnezzar became like a wild beast. It is interesting that according to

Missler in his Expositional Commentary on Daniel in 1946, Dr. Raymond Harrison observed a mental disorder like this in a man in his early twenties. The disorder lasted for five years. Doctors refer to this disease or disorder, a psychiatric state in which the patient believes he is a wolf or some other animal, as lycanthropy. This seems to fit the description of Nebuchadnezzar in verses 32 to 33.

Daniel Chapter 5

> *Belshazzar the king made a great feast for a thousand of his lords and drank wine before the thousand. Belshazzar whiles he tasted the wine, commanded to bring the golden and silver vessels which his father Nebuchadnezzar had taken out of the temple which was in Jerusalem; that the king, and his princes, his wives, and his concubines, might drink therein. Then they brought the golden vessels that were taken out of the temple of the house of God which was at Jerusalem; and the king, and his princes, his wives, and his concubines, drank in them. They drank wine and praised the gods of gold, and of silver, brass, of iron, of wood, and stone. In the same hour came forth the fingers of a man's hand, and wrote over against the candlestick upon the plaster of the wall of the king's palace, and the king saw the part of the hand that wrote. Then the king's countenance was changed, and his thoughts troubled him, so that the joints of his loins were loosed, and his knees smote one against another. The king cried aloud to bring in the astrologers, the Chaldeans, and the soothsayers. And the king spake and said to the wise men of Babylon, "Whosoever shall read this writing, and shew me the interpretation thereof, shall be clothed with scarlet, and have a chain of gold around his neck, and shall be the third ruler in the kingdom." Then came in all the king's wise men: but they could not read the writing, nor make known to the king the interpretation*

thereof. Then was King Belshazzar greatly troubled, and his countenance was changed in him, and his lords were astonished. Now the queen because of the words of the king and his lords came to the banquet house: and the queen spake and said, O king, live forever! Let not thy thoughts trouble thee, nor let thy countenance be changed: There is a man in thy kingdom, in whom is the spirit of the holy gods; and in the days of thy father light and understanding and wisdom, like the wisdom of the gods, were found in him; whom the king Nebuchadnezzar thy father, the king, I say, thy father, made master of the magicians, astrologers, Chaldeans, and soothsayers; Forasmuch as an excellent spirit, and knowledge, and understanding, interpreting of dreams, and shewing of hard sentences, and dissolving of doubts, were found in the same Daniel, whom the king named Belteshazzar: now let Daniel be called, and he will shew the interpretation. Then was Daniel brought in before the king. And the king spake and said unto Daniel, Art thou that Daniel, which art of the children of the captivity of Judah, whom the king my father brought out of Jewry? I have even heard of thee, that the spirit of the gods is in thee, and that light and understanding and excellent wisdom is found in thee. And now the wise men, the astrologers, have been brought in before me, that they should read this writing, and make known unto me the interpretation thereof: but they could not shew the interpretation of the thing: And I have heard of thee, that thou canst make interpretations, and dissolve doubts: now if thou canst read the writing, and make known to me the interpretation thereof, thou shalt be clothed with scarlet, and have a chain of gold about thy neck, and shalt be the third ruler in the kingdom. Then Daniel answered and said before the king, Let thy gifts be to thyself, and give thy rewards to another; yet I will read the writing unto the king, and make known to him the interpretation. O thou king, the highest God gave Nebuchadnezzar thy father a kingdom, and majesty, and glory, and honor And for the majesty that he gave him, all people, nations, and languages, trembled and feared before him: whom he would he slew; and whom he would he kept alive; and whom he would he set up; and whom he would he put down. But when his heart was lifted, and his mind hardened in pride, he was deposed from his kingly throne, and they took his glory from him: And he was driven from the sons of men, and heart was made like the beasts, and his dwelling was with the wild asses: they fed him with grass like oxen, and his body was wet with the dew of heaven; till he knew that the highest ruled in the kingdom of men, and that he appointeth over it whomsoever he will. And thou his son, O Belshazzar, hast not humbled thine, heart, though thou knewest all this; But hast lifted thyself against the Lord of heaven, and they have brought the vessels of his house before thee, and thou, and thy lords, thy wives, and thy concubines, have drunk wine in them; and thou hast praised the gods of silver, and gold, of brass, iron, wood, and stone, which see not, nor hear, nor know: and the God in whose hand thy breath is, and whose are all thy ways, hast thou not glorified: Then was the part of the hand sent from him; and this writing was written. And this is the writing that was written, MENE, MENE, TEKEL, UPHARSIN. This is the interpretation of the thing: MENE; God hath numbered thy kingdom and finished it. TEKEL; Thou art weighed in the balances, and art found wanting. PERES; Thy kingdom is divided, and given to the Medes and Persians. Then commanded Belshazzar, and they clothed Daniel with scarlet and put a chain of gold about his neck, and made a proclamation concerning him, that he should be the third ruler in the kingdom. On that night was Belshazzar the king of the Chaldeans slain. And Darius the Median took the kingdom, being about threescore and two years old (Dan. 5).

As we read in verse 2, Belshazzar ordered his servants to bring out the gold and silver vessels that Nebuchadnezzar had taken from the temple some seventy years earlier (see 2 Chronicles 36:18). In so doing Belshazzar was mocking the true and living God and was now seeking to worship the god of gold and pleasure. The Lord then wrote on the wall "Mene, Mene, Tekel, Upharsin." We then read that Belshazzar's countenance changed and the joints of his loins were loosed (in other words, his legs became weak and his knees knocked together).

Belshazzar was so troubled by this that he granted a reward to whoever could read the writing on the wall and interpret its meaning. When none of his staff could interpret the writing, the queen told Belshazzar about Daniel. Daniel was then sent for and met with Belshazzar. In verse 14 Belshazzar acknowledged the Spirit of God in Daniel's life along with his reputation. Belshazzar is like other nonbelievers; they have heard of the power of Christ, testimonies, and evidence of the things that the Lord has done, yet they will not accept the truth of the living God. Daniel spoke to Belshazzar and recapped the life of Nebuchadnezzar. Belshazzar knew all of these things as noted in verse 22; yet, he still wouldn't humble himself as his grandfather finally did. Daniel interpreted the meaning of the message: mene meant his days were numbered, tekel meant he was found guilty, and Upharsin meant his kingdom would be divided.

Belshazzar was slain that very night. God's judgment came upon him. God's prophecies were starting to unfold!

Let's recap a bit to get a better understanding of what the Lord has planned. We read earlier that the Jews were taken to Babylon because they broke the commandments of the Lord.

Leviticus 25:4 stated the Jews would work the land for six years and in the seventh year they would give the land a rest and not farm. They did not obey. 2 Chronicles 36:21 states the land would lay desolate for seventy years. Their disobedience is why the Jews were taken to Babylon in captivity.

Daniel, being a Bible scholar and a devoted reader of God's Word, knew that the seventy years of captivity were about to come to an end. He also knew and understood the writing on the wall. History tells us that Darius, the Mede, took control of Babylon on October 12, 539 BC, along with his general, Cyrus, the Persian, who entered the city on October 29, 539 BC. (Hence, the prophecy that stated the kingdom would be divided by the Medes and Persian empires was unfolding.) In Isaiah 45:1–7, 200 years before Cyrus's birth, our Lord called Cyrus by name and prophesied how he would take the city of Babylon. History then documented this event.

> *Thus saith the LORD to his anointed, to Cyrus, whose right hand I have holden, to subdue nations before him; and I will lose the loins of kings, to open before him the two leaved gates; and the gates shall not be shut; I will go before thee, and make the crooked places straight...that thou mayest know that I, the LORD, which call thee by thy name, am the God of Israel...I am the LORD, and there is none else. I form the light, and create darkness: I make peace, and create evil: I the LORD do all these things (Isa. 45:1–7).*

History confirms that Darius and Cyrus did take the city without any force. They backed up the river Euphrates and entered the city by the water tunnels beneath the walls. Cyrus then entered the city through the unlocked gates, which had been left open.

The writings of Josephus (Antiq. XI, I.2) confirm that Daniel showed Cyrus that God had named Isaiah 45 and appointed him to fulfill this task. Cyrus was so in awe of this that he arranged for the Jews to leave Babylon and rebuild their city. In us supported the Jews with financial incentives and military protection. Today, if you visit the British Museum, you can read the famous Cyrus Cylinder, discovered in Babylon in March 1879 where it had been placed in the foundations of the city wall soon after Cyrus's conquest of the city in 539 BC. It relates that without any battle he entered the town, sparing any calamity. "In peace, I returned to (these) sacred cities on the other side of the Tigris, the sanctuaries of which have been ruins for a long time...and established for them permanent sanctuaries. I (also) gathered all their (former) inhabitants and returned (to them) their habitations" (source: Kenneth

R. Gregg, "Cyrus the Great and the Inscription," Liberty and Power Group Blog, (http://www.hnn.us/blogs/comments/ 14171. html). This can also be found in Ezra 1:2: "Thus saith Cyrus king of Persia, The LORD God of heaven hath given me all the kingdoms of the earth; and he hath charged me to build him a house at Jerusalem, which is in Judah."

Daniel Chapter 6

Going into chapter 6 the second world leadership establishes their rule, and we find Daniel put into a position of rulership, second only to King Darius (i.e., prime minister). Daniel being a godly man was blessed by the Lord. (Other than Christ, Daniel and Joseph are the only two people in the Bible who do not state any faults against the Jewish people. Although they confessed sin in their hearts and prayed for their people, there is no mention of faults documented against them.) There are a lot of parallels between Daniel and Joseph (e.g., ability to interpret dreams, being promoted to the high post being ions, used might be guided by God, being accused by peers, etc.)

It pleased Darius Severaver the kingdom hundred and twenty princes, which should be over the whole kingdom; And over these three presidents; of whom Daniel was first: that the princes might give accounts unto them, and the king should have no damage. Then this Daniel was preferred above the presidents and princes because an excellent spirit was in him; and the king thought to set him over the whole realm. Then the presidents and princes sought to find occasion against Daniel concerning the kingdom, but they could find none occasion nor fault; forasmuch as he was faithful, neither was there any error or fault found in him. Then said these men, We shall not find any occasion against this Daniel, except we find it against him concerning the law of his God. Then these presidents and princes assembled to the king, and said thus unto him, King Darius, live forever. All the presidents of the kingdom, the governors, and the pes, the counselors, counselorstains have consulted together to establish a royal statute, and to make a firm decree, that whosoever shall ask a petition of any God or man for thirty days, save of thee, O king, he shall be cast into the den of lions. Now, O king, establish the decree, and sign the writing, that it be not changed, according to the law of the Medes and Persians, which altereth not. Wherefore king Darius signed the writing and the decree. Now when Daniel knew that the writing was signed, he went into his house; and his windows being open in his chamber toward Jerusalem, he kneeled upon his knees three times a day, prayed, and gave thanks before his God, as he did aforetime. Then these men assembled and found Daniel praying and making supplication before his God. Then they came near, and spake before the king concerning the king's decree; Hast thou not signed a decree, that every man that shall ask a petition of any God or man within thirty days, save of thee, O king, shall be cast into the den of lions? The king answered and said, The thing is true, according to the law of the Medes and Persians, which altereth not. Then answered they and said before the king, That Daniel, which is of the children of the captivity of Judah, regardeth not thee, O king, nor the decree that thou hast signed, but maketh his petition three times a day. Then the king, when he heard these words, was sore displeased with himself, and set his heart on Daniel to deliver him: and labored till the going down of the sun to deliver him. Then these men assembled unto the king, and said unto the king, Know, O king, that the law of the Medes and Persians is, That no decree nor statute which the king establisheth may be changed. Then the king commanded, and they brought Daniel and cast him into the den of lions. Now the king spake and said unto Daniel, Thy God whom thou servest continually, he will deliver thee. And a stone was brought, and laid upon the mouth of the den, and the king sealed it with his own, and with the signet of his lords; that the purpose might not be changed concerning Daniel. Then the king went to his palace, and passed the night fasting: neither were instruments of musick brought before him: and his sleep went from him. Then the king arose very early in the morning and went in haste unto the den of lions. And when he came to the den, he cried with a lamentable voice unto Daniel: and the king spake and said to Daniel, O Daniel, servant of the living God, is thy God, whom thou servest continually, able to deliver thee from the lions? Then said Daniel unto the king, O king, live forever. My God hath sent his angel, and hath shut the lions' mouths, that they have not hurt me: forasmuch as before him innocency was found in me; and also before thee, O king, have I done no hurt. Then was the king exceedingly glad for him, and commanded that they should take Daniel up out of the den. So Daniel was taken up out of the den, and no manner of hurt was found upon him because he believed in his God. And the king commanded, and they brought those men which had accused Daniel, and they cast them into the den of lions, them, their children, and their wives; and the lions had the mastery of them, and brake all their bones in pieces or ever they came at the bottom of the den. Then King Darius wrote unto all people, nations, and languages, that dwell in all the earth; Peace be multiplied unto you. I make a decree, That in every dominion of my kingdom, men tremble and fear before the God of Daniel: for he is the living God, and steadfast forever, and his kingdom that which shall not be destroyed, and his dominion shall be even unto the end. He delivereth and rescue, and he worketh signs and wonders in heaven and earth, who hath delivered Daniel from the power of the lions. So this Daniel prospered in the reign of Darius, and in the reign of Cyrus the Persian (Dan. 6).

From the text, we know that Daniel was a blessed man and God was with him. We find that Daniel's peers were envious of him and plotted against him. This is a typical satanic tactic— to plot against believers and try to tear them down. Note that Daniel knew of the king's decree; still, he chose to continue to worship his Lord regularly.

There are a few special things to point out about Daniel. First, Daniel was in his mid to late eighties, and he still obeyed the laws of worship. Three times each day he would kneel and face Jerusalem to pray. Secondly, despite the decree, Daniel had full and obedient trust in the Lord. He had walked with the Lord for nearly ninety years, and he did not fear mankind. He took a stand and worshiped God openly despite the decree. Just imagine the faith and trust Daniel had. if only we as believers in this day and age would take a firm stand with a strong devotion to our Lord! We seem to get caught up in the flesh and the problems of this world instead of heeding the will of the Spirit. As the Bible puts it, "The spirit indeed is willing, but the flesh is weak"(Matt. 26:41).

More Christians need to pray and ask our Lord Jesus Christ to give us a heart and spirit like Daniel's.

Moving on, we read that Darius was saddened when he found out Daniel was found guilty of breaking the decree.

The king was so troubled that he could not sleep. Yet, he knew of the power of Daniel's God and believed that Daniel would be spared from the lions. At this time, Darius was not a believer. However, in the morning, he hurried to Daniel, calling out Daniel's name, anticipating that Daniel would be spared. Daniel lived his life in fear of God and no one else. He purposed in his heart to worship the true and living God, and the Lord was always with him. In verses 25 to 27, we then read that Darius acknowledged to the world that the God of Daniel is the true and living God, who saves His people. Now we have had Nebuchadnezzar, Cyrus, and Darius proclaim the power of the true and living God. Daniel continued to prosper in the kingdom.

Shouldn't we as believers have the same faith? After all, we have the Bible, the evidence of the Holy Spirit working in our lives ,and His sure Word that predicts the future. Yet we do not grab hold of His promises; we struggle to let Him take complete control of our lives.

Daniel Chapter 7

This goes back in time to when Belshazzar was still in control (it occurs between chapters 4 and 5 chronologically). Although chapters 1 to 6 are mostly narrative about Daniel's career and rise to power, and chapters 7 to 12 are more about visions and dreams, chapters 2 to 7 are unique because they lay out Gentile history, past and future, from the perspective of Israel. Chapter 7 is from God's perspective. Daniel gives us a summary of the dream (verses 2 to 27), and then the interpretation is given.

In the first year of Belshazzar king of Babylon Daniel had a dream and visions of his head upon his bed: then he wrote the dream and told the sum of the matters. Daniel spake and said, I saw in my vision by night, and, behold, the four winds of the heaven strove upon the great sea. And four great beasts came up from the sea, diverse one from another. The first was like a lion, and had eagle's wings: I beheld till the wings thereof were plucked, and it was lifted from the earth, and made stand upon the feet as a man, and a man's heart was given to it. And behold another beast, a second, like to a bear, and it raised on one side, and it had three ribs in the mouth of it between the teeth of it: and they said thus unto it, Arise, devour much flesh. After this I beheld, and lo another, like a leopard, which had upon the back of it four wings of a fowl; the beast had also four heads; and dominion was given to it. After this I saw in the night visions, and behold a fourth beast, dreadful, and strong exceedingly; and it had great iron teeth: it devoured and brake in pieces, and stamped the residue with the feet of it: and it was diverse from all the beasts that were before it; and it had , dorns. I considered the horns, and, behold, there came up among them another little horn, before whom there were three of the first horns plucked up by the roots: and, behold, in this horn were eyes like the eyes of man, and a mouth speaking great things. I beheld till the thrones were cast down, and the Ancient of days did sit, whose garment was white as snow, and the hair of his head like the pure wool: his throne was like the fiery flame, and his wheels as burning fire. A fiery stream issued and came forth from before him: thousand thousands unto him, and ten thousand times ten thousand stood before him: the judgment was set, and the books were opened. I beheld then because of the voice of the great words which the horn spake: I beheld even till the beast was slain, and his body destroyed and given to the burning flame. As concerning the rest of the beasts, they had their dominion taken away: yet their lives were prolonged for a season and time. I saw in the night visions, and, behold, one like the Son of man came with the clouds of heaven, and came to the Ancient of days, and they brought him near before him. And there was given him dominion, and glory, and a kingdom, that all people, nations, and languages, should serve him: his dominion is an everlasting dominion, which shall not pass away, and his kingdom that which shall not be destroyed. I Daniel was grieved in my spirit amid my body, and the visions of my head troubled me. I came near unto one of them that stood by and asked him the truth of all this. So he told me and made me know the interpretation of the things. These great beasts, which are four, are four kings, which shall arise out of the earth. But the saints of the highest shall take the kingdom, and possess the kingdom forever, even forever and ever. Then I would know the truth of the fourth beast, which was diverse from all the others, exceeding dreadful, whose teeth were of iron, and his nails of brass; which devoured, brake in pieces, and stamped the residue with his feet; And of the ten horns that were in his head, and of the other which came up, and before whom three fell; even of that horn that had eyes, and a mouth that spake very great things, whose look was stouter than his fellows. I beheld, and the same horn made war with the saints and prevailed against them; Until the Ancient of days came, and judgment was given to the saints of the highest; and the time came that the saints possessed the kingdom. Thus he said, The fourth beast shall be the fourth kingdom upon earth, which shall be diverse from all kingdoms, and shall devour the whole earth, and shall tread it down, and break it in pieces. And the ten horns out of this kingdom are ten kings that shall arise: and another shall rise after them, and he shall be diverse from the first, and he shall subdue three kings. And he shall speak great words against the highest, and shall wear out the saints of the highest, and think to change times and laws: and they shall be given into his hand until a time and times and the dividing of time. But the judgment shall sit, and they shall take away his dominion, to consume and to destroy it unto the end. And the kingdom and dominion, and the greatness of the kingdom under the whole heaven, shall be given to the people of the saints of the highest, whose kingdom is an everlasting kingdom, and all dominions shall serve and obey him. Hitherto is the end of the matter. As for me Daniel, my cogitations much troubled me, and my countenance changed in me: but I kept the matter in my heart (Dan. 7).

Here we have read about four great beasts representing the four world kingdoms. First is the lion, which is a symbol for Babylon (see Jer. 4:7 and Jer. 50:17). The "man's heart" that "was given to it" could perhaps be a reference to King Nebuchadnezzar acknowledging God. Next, we have the bear, which symbolizes the Medes and the Persians joining forces to conquer Babylon under Darius and Cyrus. The third kingdom was the leopard, which represents Alexander the Great and his Grecian empire. The four heads of the vision represent Alexander's four generals—Casandra, Lasimakas, Salukes, and Talame. It is also interesting to note that a lion devours, a bear crushes, and a leopard springs upon its prey. As we look back at the history of these empires, we will find these same similarities in their quests to conquer.

Last in line is the fourth beast, unlike any of the other beasts. This beast represents the Roman Empire, which was the last world ruler on earth and is prophesied to rise again. History shows the Roman Empire was not defeated (as noted previously); it was divided (as represented by the legs of iron) by Diocletian in AD 284. It broke up in AD 476 and fell apart within itself, represented by the toes (a mixture of iron and clay, representing stronger and weaker nations).

Here in chapter 7, Daniel emphasizes the feet that trampled the residue of the nations. If we compare this with Daniel 2, we read that in later days the feet or toes unite together and become one. We now believe this is a reference to the establishment of the European Union, which is gaining in strength. Daniel prophesied that out of this Roman Empire would come a world superpower that would set up a one-world government and assign kings to certain regions of the world. Next, a charismatic leader would emerge and take control of the world while speaking blasphemy against the true and living God.

We can also read about this in Revelation 13. It refers to the world leader who arises out of the Roman Empire or is of Roman descent. Then in Revelation 6, this world leader appears riding a white horse and carrying a bow (note: there is no mention of arrows). The Greek word in the text has the same meaning as the Hebrew word found in Genesis when God made a covenant with Noah with a rainbow. The rainbow was a reminder of God's covenant. Scripture tells us that this world leader comes to leadership bringing peace and prosperity. He then makes a covenant with many—for a time.

Finally, Daniel ends the chapter with the last kingdom, reigned over by our Lord and Savior, Jesus Christ. Yes, the same glorious Lord who died on the cross and shed His precious blood for the forgiveness of our sins will come back to reign on earth and sit on the throne of David (Rev. 19).

Daniel Chapter 8

Scripture states in Amos 3:7 that the Lord reveals dreams and prophecies to His servants. Daniel Chapter 8 relates Daniel's second dream. Chronologically, chapter 8 occurs about twelve years before chapter 5 and two years after chapter 7 (a bit confusing). In Daniel's dream, he finds himself in Shushan (historically, Shushan was 230 miles east of Babylon and was the home of Esther). Read on!

> In the third year of the reign of King Belshazzar a vision appeared unto me, even unto me Daniel, after that which appeared unto me at the first. And I saw in a vision; and it came to pass, when I saw, that I was at Shushan in the palace, which is in the province of Elam; and I saw in a vision, and I was by the river of Ulai. Then I lifted my eyes, and saw, and, behold, there stood before the river a ram which had two horns: and the two horns were high, but one was higher than the other, and the higher came up last. I saw the ram pushing westward, and northward, and southward; so that no beasts might stand before him, neither was there any that could deliver out of his hand; but he did according to his will, and became great. And as I was considering, behold, the goat came from the west on the face of the whole earth, and touched not the ground: and the goat had a notable horn between his eyes. And he came to the ram that had two horns, which I had seen standing before the river, and ran unto him in the fury of his power. And I saw him come close unto the ram, and he was moved with choler against him, and smote the ram, and brake his two horns: and there was no power in the ram to stand before him, but he cast him down to the ground, and stamped upon him: and there was none that could deliver the ram out of his hand. Therefore the goat waxed very great: and when he was strong, the great horn was broken; and for it came up four notable ones toward the four winds of heaven. And out of one of them

came forth a little horn, which waxed exceeding great, toward the south, and the east, and the pleasant land. And it waxed great, even to the host of heaven; and it cast down some of the hosts and of the stars to the ground, and stamped upon them. Yea, he magnified himself even to the prince of the host, and by him, the daily sacrifice was taken away, and the place of the sanctuary was cast down. And a host was given him against the daily sacrifice because of transgression, and it cast down the truth to the ground, and it practiced, and prospered. Then I heard one saint speaking, and another saint said unto that certain saint which spake, How long shall be the vision concerning the daily sacrifice, and the transgression of desolation, to give both the sanctuary and the host to be trodden under foot? And he said unto me, Unto two thousand and three hundred days; then shall the sanctuary be cleansed. And it came to pass, when I, even I Daniel, had seen the vision, and sought for the meaning, then, behold, there stood before me as the appearance of a man. And I heard a man's voice between the banks of Ulai, which called and said, Gabriel, make this man understand the vision. So he came near where I stood: and when he came, I was afraid, and fell upon my face: but he said unto me, Understand, O son of man: for at the time of the end shall be the vision. Now as he was speaking with me, I was in a deep sleep on my face toward the ground: but he touched me, and set me upright. And he said Behold, I will make thee know what shall be in the last end of the indignation: for at the time appointed the end shall be. The ram which thou sawest having two horns are the kings of Media and Persia. And the rough goat is the king of Grecia: and the great horn that is between his eyes is the first king. Now that being broken, whereas four stood up for it, four kingdoms shall stand up out of the nation, but not in his power. And in the latter time of their kingdom, when the transgressors are come to the full, a king of fierce countenance, and understanding dark sentences, shall stand up. And his power shall be mighty, but not by his power: and he shall destroy wonderfully, and shall prosper, and practiced shall destroy the mighty and the holy people. And through his policy also he shall cause craft to prosper in his hand, and he shall magnify himself in his heart, and by peace shall destroy many: he shall also stand up against the Prince of princes, but he shall be broken without hand. And the vision of the evening and the morning which was told is true: wherefore shut thou up the vision; for it shall be for many days. And I Daniel fainted, and was sick certain days; afterward, I rose, and did the king's business; and I was astonished at the vision, but none understood it (Dan. 8).

In Daniel's vision, we have our first appearance in the Bible of the angel known as Gabriel. (Note: Gabriel is always the messenger, and Michael is the warrior.) Gabriel told Daniel that he would interpret the dream for him. Gabriel then spoke of the rise of the Medes and the Persians, who would overthrow Babylon ten years later. He continued to foretell of the Grecian Empire that would rise to power 200-plus years later to overthrow the Medes and the Persians. The Grecian Empire would be led by Alexander the Great in 334 BC (represented by the large horn), who died at an early age; his kingdom was then divided between his four generals.

Next, Gabriel spoke about the fourth kingdom, which will come back to power and be controlled by demonic powers (verse 24); this charismatic leader will be known as the Antichrist, and he will deceive many until his kingdom is broken, but not by human hands. This refers to Jesus Christ's return to the earth with his saints (that's us, the true believers) as noted in Revelation 19. Then Daniel is told to seal up the vision, for it is about many days in the future.

As believers, we often ask the Lord for a sign of His presence, for reassurance or confirmation of His will in our lives, or for sign evidence. His Word, the Holy Scriptures, have been given to us so that we should not be ignorant of His power. God continued to foretell the past, present, and future with 100 percent accuracy. And yet, we still ask for a sign. We say, "Lord, show me, and I will believe." The Lord answers, "Believe, and I will show you!" The Lord has told us all things from beginning to end, from Genesis to Revelation. Still, we often falter in our faith.

Yes, we are aware of how hard it is to be in this world and yet not of this world. Sometimes we get so caught up in our daily routines and our fleshly selves that we forget about His promises and our life in His eternal presence. Think back to our founding fathers in the United States. They read their Bibles and believed in God's promises. These faith-based brothers demonstrated true strength of faith to dare to build a nation on "In God we trust"! The laws of our land were based on the Ten Commandments, and the people chose to fear God and live by His Word.

Daniel Chapter 9

Chapter 9 of Daniel is known as the seventy weeks of Daniel. It foretells the first and second coming of Christ to the exact day. Now keep in mind when our Lord said "of that day and hour knoweth no man" (Matt. 24:36), He was referring to the Rapture of the Church. This is an event that is a mystery, and no exact time frame is given. The Rapture is when Christ comes for His Church (1 Thess. 4:15; 1 Cor. 15:51–53); whereas in the Second Coming, Christ comes with His church (Rev. 19:11–16). Here we are told of the first advent of Christ when Christ is to ride into Jerusalem (the Triumphant Entree). Daniel 9:25–26 states there are 69 X 7 years, or 483 years, from the time the decree is sent out to rebuild the walls of Jerusalem until the Prince shall come. In Nehemiah 2:1–9,

Artaxerxes signed the decree in the month of Nisan (in 445 BC) and supplied Nehemiah with guards, funds, and materials to go and rebuild the wall (this decree is also part of historic records), which puts Christ riding in on a donkey on the ninth of Nisan in AD 32. (Read Sir Robert Anderson's The Coming Prince for more details.) Christ wept in Luke 19:41–42, stating, "Oh, Jerusalem, if you had only known that this was your day" (author's paraphrase). If only the Jews would have read their Scriptures, then they would have known that this day was arranged and foretold. Also, from this point on blindness covers the eyes of the Jews until the fullness of the Gentiles comes to pass (Rom. 11:25). As stated in Daniel 12:11, when the world leader stops the sacrifices in the temple during his reign, there will be 1,290 days until Christ returns with His Church.

> *In the first year of Darius the son of Ahasuerus, of the seed of the Medes, which was made king over the realm of the Chaldeans; In the first year of his reign I Daniel understood by books the number of the years, whereof the word of the LORD came to Jeremiah the prophet, that he would accomplish seventy years in the desolations of Jerusalem. And I set my face unto the Lord God, to seek by prayer and supplications, with fasting, and sackcloth, and ashes: And I prayed unto the LORD my God, and made my confession, and said, O Lord, the great and dreadful God, keeping the covenant and mercy to them that love him, and to them that keep his commandments; We have sinned, and have committed iniquity, and have done wickedly, and have rebelled, even by departing from thy precepts and thy judgments: Neither have we hearkened unto thy servants the prophets, which spake in thy name to our kings, our princes, and our fathers, and to the people of the land. O LORD, righteousness belongeth unto thee, but unto us confusion of faces, as at this day; to the men of Judah, to*

the inhabitants of Jerusalem, and unto all Israel, that are near, and that are far off, through all the countries whither thou hast driven them, because of their trespass that they have trespassed against thee. O Lord, to us belongeth confusion of face, to our kings, to our princes, and our fathers, because we have sinned against thee. To the Lord our God belong mercies and forgiveness we have rebelled against him; Neither have we obeyed the voice of the LORD our God, to walk in his laws, which he set before us by his servants the prophets. Yea, all Israel have transgressed thy law, even by departing, that they might not obey thy voice; therefore the curse is poured upon us, and the oath that is written in the law of Moses the servant of God, because we have sinned against him. And he hath confirmed his words, which he spake against us, and against our jthees that judged us, by bringing upon us a great evil: for under the whole heaven hath not been done as hath been done upon Jerusalem. As it is written in the law of Moses, all this evil comes upon us: yet made we not our prayer before the LORD our God, that we might turn from our iniquities, and understand thy truth. Therefore hath the LORD watched upon the evil, and brought it upon us: for the LORD our God is righteous in all his works which he doeth: for we obeyed not his voice. And now, O Lord our God, that hast brought thy people forth out of the land of Egypt with a mighty hand, and hast gotten thee renown, as at this day; we have sinned, we have done wickedly. O LORD, according to all thy righteousness, I beseech thee, let thine anger and thy fury beisurned away from thy city Jerusalem, thy holy mountain: because for our sins, and the iniquities of our fathers, Jerusalem and, thy people are become a reproach to all that are about us. Now therefore, O our God, hear the prayer of thy servant, and his supplications, and cause thy face to shine upon thy desolate sanctuary, for the

Lord's sake. O my God, incline thine ear, and hear; open thine eyes, and behold our desolations, and the city which is called by thy name: for we do not present our supplications before thee for our righteousnesses, but for thy great mercies. O Lord, hear; O Lord, forgive; O Lord, hearken and do; defer not, for thine own sake, O my God: for thy city and thy people are called by thy name. And whiles I was speaking, and praying, and confessing my sin and the sin of my people Israel, and presenting my supplication before the LORD my God for the holy mountain of my God; Yea, whiles I was speaking in prayer, even the man Gabriel, whom I had seen in the vision at the beginning, being caused to fly swiftly, touched me about the time of the evening oblation. And he informed me and talked with me, and said, O Daniel, I now come forth to give thee skill and understanding. At the beginning of thy supplications the commandment came forth, and I am come to shew thee; for thou art greatly beloved: therefore understand the matter, and consider the vision. Seventy weeks are determined upon thy people and thy holy city, to finish the transgression, and to make an end of sins, and to make reconciliation for iniquity, and to bring in everlasting righteousness, and to seal up the vision and prophecy, and to anoint the most Holy. Know therefore and understand, that from the going forth of the commandment to restore and to build Jerusalem unto the Messiah the Prince shall be seven weeks, and threescore and two weeks: the street shall be built again, and the wall, even in troublous times. And after threescore and two weeks shall Messiah be cut off, but not for himself: and the people of the prince that shall come shall destroy the city and the sanctuary; and the end thereof shall be with a flood, and unto the end of the war desolations are determined. And he shall confirm the covenant with many for one week: and in the amidek he shall cause the sacrifice and the oblation to cease, and for the overspreading of abominations he shall make it desolate, even until the consummation, and that determined shall be poured upon the desolate (Dan. 9).

Chronologically, Daniel 9 would fit in one year after Belshazzar's feast in chapter 5, for that was the first year of Darius's reign. Daniel studied the Word of God, and he understood that the seventy weeks (or years) were ending. Daniel lived, believed, and hid the Word in his heart, confessing his sins and the sins of his people. Verse 21 is about the time of the evening offering. There had not been an offering or a temple for over seventy years, yet Daniel still remembered from his youth the times and procedures to offer his worship to the true and living God. Gabriel again appeared to Daniel, and this time, in verse 23, he called Daniel "beloved." This is very interesting, because John was referred to as "one of his disciples, whom Jesus loved" (John 13:23). John the Beloved received the Book of Revelation, and Daniel the Beloved received these Old Testament prophecies. The two books are parallel in many ways.

The next prediction is the seventy weeks spoken of in verse 24. Gabriel told Daniel that six things were determined for the Jews and the Holy City. Three of these six have been fulfilled in the first sixty-nine weeks (or weeks of years). The last week (or the last seven-year period) is yet to come. The first three were accomplished by Christ, who came down to earth, died for our sins, and rose from the dead. The last three periods will be accomplished when Christ returns with His Church and sets up His millennial reign.

Daniel Chapter 10

This is a prelude and introduction for chapters 11 and 12. Of interest in this chapter is the insight into the spiritual realm and the rankings of angels. Let's read on!

In the third year of Cyrus king of Persia, a thing was revealed unto Daniel, whose name was called Belteshazzar; and the thing was true, but the time appointed was long: and he understood the thing, and had an understanding of the vision. In those days Daniel was mourning three full weeks. I ate no pleasant bread, neither came flesh nor wine in my mouth, neither did I anoint myself at all, till three whole weeks were fulfilled. And in the four and twentieth day of the first month, as I was by the side of the great river, which is Hiddekel; Then I lifted my eyes, and looked, and behold a certain man clothed in linen, whose loins were girded with fine gold of Uphaz: His body also was like the beryl, and his face as the appearance of lightning, and his eyes as lamps of fire, and his arms and his feet like in color to polished brass, and the voice of his words like the voice of a multitude. And I Daniel alone saw the vision: for the men that were with me saw not the vision; but a great quaking fell upon them so that they fled to hide. Therefore I was left alone, and saw this great vision, and there remained no strength in me: for my comeliness was turned in me into corruption, and I retained no strength. Yet heard I the voice of his words: and when I heard the voice of his words, then was I in a deep sleep on my face, and my face toward the ground. And, behold, an hand touched me, which set me upon my knees and upon the palms of my hands. And he said unto me, O Daniel, a man greatly beloved, understand the words that I speak unto thee, and stand upright: for unto thee am I now sent. And when he had spoken this word unto me, I stood trembling. Then said he unto me, Fear not, Daniel: for from the first day that thou didst set thine heart to understand, and to chasten thyself before thy God, thy words were heard, and I am come for thy words. But the prince of the kingdom of Persia withstood me one and twenty days: but, lo, Michael, one of the chief princes, came to help me; and I remained there with the kings of Persia. Now I am come to make thee understand what shall befall thy people in the latter days: for yet the vision is for many days. And when he had spoken such words unto me, I set my face toward the ground, and I became dumb. And, behold, one like the similitude of the sons of men touched my lips: then I opened my mouth, and spake, and said unto him that stood before me, O my lord, by the vision my sorrows are turned upon me, and I have retained no strength. For how can the servant of this my lord talk with this my lord? for as for me, straightway there remained no strength in me, neither is there breath left in me. Then there came again and touched me one like the appearance of a man, and he strengthened me, And said, O man greatly beloved, fear not: peace be unto thee, be strong, yea, be strong. And when he had spoken unto me, I was strengthened, and said, Let my lord speak; for thou hast strengthened me. Then said he, Knowest thou wherefore I come unto thee? and now will I return to fight with the prince of Persia: and when I am gone forth, lo, the prince of Grecia shall come. But I will shew thee that which is noted in the Scripture of truth: and there is none that holdeth with me in these things, but Michael your prince (Dan. 10).

This chapter starts off with a historical background of the reign of Cyrus. Later it speaks of the future empire (the Grecian Empire, verse 20) that would come to power hundreds of years later. This godly man, Daniel, was about ninety years old, likely retired from his political office, and unable to travel to Jerusalem to worship (most likely due to age and health). In the first month, which would be Nisan or Passover, Daniel fasted for three weeks. He started fasting on the 3rd of Nisan and finished on the 24th. (Note: when the Holy Spirit gives us specific dates in the Bible, there is a significant reason.) Daniel went to the Tigris River, where he lifted up his eyes and saw a vision. Those around him did not see the vision, although something terrified them, so they left. This parallels Paul's experience on the road to Damascus when he encountered Christ.

The vision given to Daniel by Jesus Christ seems very similar to the vision John had of Christ in Revelation 1:12–17:

> *And I turned to see the voice that spake with me. And being turned, I saw seven golden candlesticks; And in the midst of the seven candlesticks one like unto the Son of man, clothed with a garment down to the foot, and girt about the paps with a golden girdle. His head and his hairs were white like wool, as white as snow; and his eyes were as a flame of fire; And his feet like unto fine brass, as if they burned in a furnace; and his voice as the sound of many waters. And he had in his right hand seven stars: and out of his mouth went a sharp two-edged sword: and his countenance was as the sun shineth in his strength. And when I saw him, I fell at his feet as dead. And he laid his right hand upon me, saying unto me, Fear not; I am the first and the last (Rev. 1:12–17).*

After Daniel saw the vision of Christ, he fell down without strength. An angel came and touched Daniel and comforted him. Scholars believe this angel was Gabriel. The angel went on to say when Daniel humbled himself and first started praying his prayers were heard and the angel was dispatched. However, the mighty powers of the Prince of Persia (meaning Satan or one of his high-ranking demons) detained this angel, and the mighty archangel Michael was called in to release the angel so that he could get to Daniel.

What I like most about the Bible is that it gives us insight on what is going on around us. No matter what situation we are facing, the Bible can comfort us with the story of a similar experience. Here we have an insight into the spiritual realm, the ranking of powers and forces. Let's not forget about the book of Job where Satan had access to God's throne and we can read the dialogue between Satan and God in regards to Job. In this passage, we are assured that the Lord will never give us more then we can handle; in fact, He is always there watching over and protecting us. Although as Christians, we are promised trials and tribulation in this world, we do have the promise that He has overcome this world and the things of this world (John 16:33). Abiding in Christ gives us the power to live for eternity. In Ephesians 6, we get another glimpse of spiritual warfare, the ranking of Satan's demons. Then, more importantly, is what we must do for protection—put on the armor of God.

Getting back to Daniel, the day that Daniel started praying, an angel was sent to comfort him and answer his prayer, but the angel was held back or detained by the demonic spiritual realm. This gives us great insight into the battles that are going on around us even now and how Satan tries to hinder our prayer life and relationship with the Lord. We know that our prayers are heard and action is being taken, but sometimes... Our Lord is all-knowing; still, the key to all of our prayers is to "Trust in the LORD with all your heart, And lean not on your own understanding; in all your ways acknowledge Him, And He shall direct your paths" (Prov. 3:5–6 NKJV).

Also pray for His will to be done in our lives. It is imperative to keep God's promises hidden in our heart, like Romans 8:28, which assures us: "All things work together for good to those who love God, to those who are the called according to His purpose" (NKJV).

Keep in mind that prayer is not getting God to do what we want; prayer is a relationship with our Father, asking Him to let His will be done in our lives. He knows our hearts, thoughts and desires; and if our will is in line with His will, He will give us the desires of our hearts.

Daniel was never selfish in prayer; he was obedient to the will of God. He not only prayed for himself and confessed his sins, he also did so for the people. It was never about Daniel; it was always about his servanthood to the Lord. This may be why Daniel received such visions and had such a beautiful relationship with the Lord. If our prayers are not answered right away, it may be because of our selfishness or there is spiritual warfare in the angelic realm, or perhaps the Lord has a better plan and is delaying His work to fulfill His perfect plan in our lives.

Remember that when Lazarus was sick, the word was sent to the Lord to come and heal him. The Lord delayed. Mary and Martha were angry, hurt, upset, and let down. The Lord had a better plan that necessitated Lazarus dying. Yes, He tested the sisters' faith. Instead of a healing, He performed a resurrection (see John 11). Our God is awesome, and all things are possible through Jesus Christ. It may be best summed up in Genesis 1:1: "In the beginning God created the heaven and the earth."

"In the beginning, God..." The first sentence of the Bible tells us of His eternal deity—His omniscience, His omnipresence and His omnipotence. Then Christ's last words in the book of Revelation refer to the ending—His return. "Surely I come quickly" (Rev. 22:20). That's right—the Great "I Am" of the Bible is returning!

To sum up the tenth chapter, we have history giving us the time frame as the third year of Cyrus (534 BC); Daniel fasting in prayer for twenty-one days; a vision of Jesus Christ; an angel sent to Daniel yet detained by demonic forces; Michael the archangel interceding; Daniel being strengthened by the angel; Daniel the Beloved being highly esteemed by God; a glimpse of the next empire to come—the Grecian Empire; and finally a passage that refers to "the Scripture of truth," which is the Word of God, and the vision that will be given to Daniel in chapter 11.

Daniel Chapter 11

Continuing, we discover that chapter 11 fills in some of the details of chapter 9 and it gives us more details of the last three of the four world empires found in Daniel 2 as well as the beast in chapter 7. Chapter 11 takes the image and the beast and now gives us a clearer picture of them, yet this time we see them as nations. In these thirty-five verses we have the details of the major rulers of the Persian Empire as well as the third empire, headed by Alexander the Great, who died and left his four generals to divide up the regions. It starts out with Darius the Mede (539 BC) and concludes with Antioch Epiphanes (175–164 BC). It is interesting that between verses 11 and 35 we do not read of the fourth empire. The Roman Empire is skipped, and verse 36 goes right to the last world leader—the Antichrist, who comes out of the Roman Empire or of Roman descent. Let's continue!

> *Also, I, in the first year of Darius the Mede, even I, stood to confirm and to strengthen him. And now will I shew thee the truth. Behold, there shall stand up yet three kings in Persia; and the fourth shall be far richer than they all: and by his strength through his riches he shall stir up all against the realm of Grecia. And a mighty king shall stand up, that shall rule with great dominion, and do according to his will. And when he shall stand up, his kingdom shall be broken, and shall be divided toward the four winds of heaven; and not to his posterity, nor according to his dominion which he ruled: for his kingdom shall be plucked up, even for others beside those. And the king of the south shall be strong, and one of his princes; and he shall be strong above him, and have dominion; his dominion shall be a great*

dominion. And in the end of years they shall join themselves together; for the king's daughter of the south shall come to the king of the north to make an agreement: but she shall not retain the power of the arm; neither shall he stand, nor his arm: but she shall be given up, and they that brought her, and he that begat her, and he that strengthened her in these times. But out of a branch of her roots shall one stand up in his estate, which shall come with an army, and shall enter into the fortress of the king of the north, and shall deal against them, and shall prevail: And shall also carry captives into Egypt their gods, with their princes, and with their precious vessels of silver and of gold; and he shall continue more years than the king of the north. So the king of the south shall come into his kingdom, and shall return into his own land. But his sons shall be stirred up, and shall assemble a multitude of great forces: and one shall certainly come, and overflow, and pass through: then shall he return, and be stirred up, even to his fortress. And the king of the south shall be moved with choler, and shall come forth and fight with him, even with the king of the north: and he shall set forth a great multitude; but the multitude shall be given into his hand. And when he hath taken away the multitude, his heart shall be lifted up; and he shall cast down many ten thousands: but he shall not be strengthened by it. For the king of the north shall return, and shall set forth a multitude greater than the former, and shall certainly come after certain years with a great army and with much riches. And in those times there shall many stand up against the king of the south: also the robbers of thy people shall exalt themselves to establish the vision; but they shall fall. So the king of the north shall come, and cast up a mount, and take the most fenced cities: and the arms of the south shall not withstand, neither his chosen people, neither shall there be any strength to withstand.

But he that cometh against him shall do according to his own will, and none shall stand before him: and he shall stand in the glorious land, which by his hand shall be consumed. He shall also set his face to enter with the strength of his whole kingdom, and upright ones with him; thus shall he do: and he shall give him the daughter of women, corrupting her: but she shall not stand on his side, neither be for him. After this shall he turn his face unto the isles, and shall take many: but a prince for his own behalf shall cause the reproach offered by him to cease; without his own reproach he shall cause it to turn upon him. Then he shall turn his face toward the fort of his own land: but he shall stumble and fall, and not be found. Then shall stand up in his estate a raiser of taxes in the glory of the kingdom: but within few days he shall be destroyed, neither in anger, nor in battle. And in his estate shall stand up a vile person, to whom they shall not give the honour of the kingdom: but he shall come in peaceably, and obtain the kingdom by flatteries. And with the arms of a flood shall they be overflown from before him, and shall be broken; yea, also the prince of the covenant. And after the league made with him he shall work deceitfully: for he shall come up, and shall become strong with a small people. He shall enter peaceably even upon the fattest places of the province; and he shall do that which his fathers have not done, nor his fathers' fathers; he shall scatter among them the prey, and spoil, and riches: yea, and he shall forecast his devices against the strong holds, even for a time. And he shall stir up his power and his courage against the king of the south with a great army; and the king of the south shall be stirred up to battle with a very great and mighty army; but he shall not stand: for they shall forecast devices against him. Yea, they that feed of the portion of his meat shall destroy him, and his army shall overflow: and many shall fall down slain. And both of these kings' hearts shall be to do mischief, and they shall speak lies at one table; but it shall not prosper: for yet the end shall be at the time appointed. Then shall he return into his land with great riches; and his heart shall be against the holy covenant; and he shall do exploits, and return to his own land. At the time appointed he shall return, and come toward the south; but it shall not be as the former, or as the latter. For the ships of Chittim shall come against him: therefore he shall be grieved, and return, and have indignation against the holy covenant: so shall he do; he shall even return, and have intelligence with them that forsake the holy covenant. And arms shall stand on his part, and they shall pollute the sanctuary of strength, and shall take away the daily sacrifice, and they shall place the abomination that maketh desolate. And such as do wickedly against the covenant shall he corrupt by flatteries: but the people that do know their God shall be strong, and do exploits. And they that understand among the people shall instruct many: yet they shall fall by the sword, and by flame, by captivity, and by spoil, many days. Now when they shall fall, they shall be helped with a little help: but many shall cleave to them with flatteries. And some of them of understanding shall fall, to try them, and to purge, and to make them white, even to the time of the end: because it is yet for a time appointed. And the king shall do according to his will; and he shall exalt himself, and magnify himself above every god, and shall speak marvellous things against the God of gods, and shall prosper till the indignation be accomplished: for that that is determined shall be done. Neither shall he regard the God of his fathers, nor the desire of women, nor regard any god: for he shall magnify himself above all. But in his estate shall he honour the God of forces: and a god whom his fathers knew not shall he honour with gold, and silver, and with precious stones, and pleasant things. Thus shall he do in the strongest holds with a strange god, whom he shall acknowledge and increase with glory: and he shall cause them to rule over many, and shall divide the land for gain. And at the time of the end shall the king of the south push at him: and the king of the north shall come against him like a whirlwind, with chariots, and with horsemen, and with many ships; and he shall enter into the countries, and shall overflow and pass over. He shall enter also into the glorious land, and many countries shall be overthrown: but these shall escape out of his hand, even Edom, and Moab, and the chief of the children of Ammon. He shall stretch forth his hand also upon the countries: and the land of Egypt shall not escape. But he shall have power over the treasures of gold and of silver, and over all the precious things of Egypt: and the Libyans and the Ethiopians shall be at his steps. But tidings out of the east and out of the north shall trouble him: therefore he shall go forth with great fury to destroy, and utterly to make away many. And he shall plant the tabernacles of his palace between the seas in the glorious holy mountain; yet he shall come to his end, and none shall help him (Dan. 11).

Let's start with verse 2, which will lay out the history of the Persian leaders. The angel said that there would be three kings and then a fourth who would have great riches. History has labeled these kings that followed Cyrus as:

1. Cambyses, 529 BC
2. Pseudo Smerdes, 522 BC
3. Darius Hystaspis, 521 BC (also mentioned in Ezra 5 and 6)
4. Xerxes, 480 BC (who went up against Greece and lost)

Verse 3 states, "And a mighty king shall stand up, that shall rule with great dominion, and do according to his will." History names this mighty king as Alexander the Great, who overthrew the Medio-Persian Empire, so Greece became the third world empire in 335 BC. Next we read that this empire stands up (or comes to power), yet it is broken and given to the four winds of the earth. History tells us that when Alexander died (at the age of thirty-two), he did not have an heir to his throne, so his kingdom was divided by his four generals:

1. Cassander, who took Macedonia
2. Lysimachus, who took Asia Minor
3. Seleucus Nicator, who took Syria and the Middle East
4. Ptolemy, who took Egypt

Next we have the southern empire, which is Egypt, headed by Ptolemy I Soter, 323 to 285 BC, starting to build an alliance with the king of the north, or Syria, headed by Seleucus I Nicator, 312 to 281 BC. At the end of [some] years the north and the south join together in marriage, when Ptolemy II Philadelphus (285 to 246 BC) gave his daughter Berenice in marriage to Antiochus Theos. From here on through the next fifteen or so verses, there are battles and rulers coming and going, up to verse 21, in which we are introduced to Antiochus Ephipanes, 175 BC. We then read in verse 31 that Antiochus places the "abomination that maketh desolate" in the temple in Jerusalem. In verse 32, we have God raising up the Maccabean revolution, which is during the time period between the Old and New Testaments. (For more information on this time period, read 1st and 2nd Maccabees in the Apocrypha.)

Most historians have tried to late-date the book of Daniel, mainly because of chapter 11 being so precise and accurate in regards to world history. These are people who cannot face the fact that our God is all-knowing and that He has given us His Word in advance. We can read Scripture and know that from Genesis to Revelation our Lord is allknowing. Instead of the Lord given us modern-day prophets, He has given us history prewritten—past, present and future. It is also interesting to note that during the Grecian rule, the whole world spoke Greek. Therefore, in order for the Jews to read and understand their Scriptures, the Old Testament was translated into Greek (this is called the Septuagint) by seventy Jewish scholars at the library in Alexandria between 285 and 270 BC. So the Septuagint (which included the book of Daniel) was in print before the events foretold in verse 6 of chapter 11 happened.

Now let's plunge into the future—that's right, things to come. Our Lord has been 100 percent accurate thus far with His Word; therefore, "by faith" choose to believe that what God says will happen will surely happen. Remember that our Lord is a loving God and does not wish for any to perish, but for all to repent and put their trust in His Son, our Lord and Savior, Jesus Christ, who shed His blood so that we may have everlasting life (see 2 Peter 3:9).

So verse 35 is the last verse of the past, and verse 36 brings in the Antichrist, the future world leader. This is the beginning of the last seven years of world history, which is ushered in by this charismatic world leader, who comes to power by seeming to bring peace and prosperity. We can also read about him in Revelation 6:2, where he is described as the rider of the white horse. The Scriptures tell us that he is loved by all for the first three and a half years of his reign, and then he shows his true colors and the nations of the world rise up against him, as seen here in verse 40 to 43. Next we read that the kings of the east come up against him (see Revelation 16:12) along with the kings of the north, and this begins to set the stage for the final battle, which will take place in the valley of Megido.

Daniel Chapter 12

Now concludes the vision that began in chapter 10. When the angel came to Daniel, he stated, "Now I am come to make thee understand what shall befall thy people [the nation of

Israel] in the latter days [the last seven years of world history, or the seventieth week of Daniel]: for yet the vision is for many days [in the future]" (Dan. 10:14).

> And at that time shall Michael stand up, the great prince which standeth for the children of thy people: and there shall be a time of trouble, such as never was since there was a nation even to that same time: and at that time thy people shall be delivered, every one that shall be found written in the book. And many of them that sleep in the dust of the earth shall awake, some to everlasting life, and some to shame and everlasting contempt. And they that be wise shall shine as the brightness of the firmament; and they that turn many to righteousness as the stars for ever and ever. But thou, O Daniel, shut up the words, and seal the book, even to the time of the end: many shall run to and fro, and knowledge shall be increased. Then I Daniel looked, and, behold, there stood other two, the one on this side of the bank of the river, and the other on that side of the bank of the river. And one said to the man clothed in linen, which was upon the waters of the river, How long shall it be to the end of these wonders? And I heard the man clothed in linen, which was upon the waters of the river, when he held up his right hand and his left hand unto heaven, and sware by him that liveth for ever that it shall be for a time, times, and an half; and when he shall have accomplished to scatter the power of the holy people, all these things shall be finished. And I heard, but I understood not: then said I, O my Lord, what shall be the end of these things? And he said, Go thy way, Daniel: for the words are closed up and sealed till the time of the end. Many shall be purified, and made white, and tried; but the wicked shall do wickedly: and none of the wicked shall understand; but the wise shall understand. And from the time that the daily sacrifice shall be taken

away, and the abomination that maketh desolate set up, there shall be a thousand two hundred and ninety days. Blessed is he that waiteth, and cometh to the thousand three hundred and five and thirty days. But go thou thy way till the end be: for thou shalt rest, and stand in thy lot at the end of the days (Dan. 12).

Here we notice that Michael, the archangel of Israel, will stand up for the people during troublesome times. These times will be like no other on the face of the earth. At the end of the time, the Just shall be delivered and shine in righteousness. We then read that Daniel is told to seal up the book until the time of the end, when knowledge shall increase and people will understand what is written. Could we be near the end? How much longer will the Lord hold back His judgment? I find it interesting that Daniel was told to seal up the book, whereas John (the writer of Revelation) is told not to the seal up His words "for the time is at hand" (Rev. 22:10). Keep in mind, we are now living in God's grace, and He promises to return for His people and to judge the unrighteous accordingly. He has given us specific signs, times and seasons, a description of the state this world will be in prior to His coming. And as is stated in the prophecies: "As it was in the days of Noah, so it will be at the coming of the Son of Man" (Matt. 24:37 NIV). So the question is, are we living and looking for Christ? The Bible states that we should be ready and anticipate His coming at any moment. The Scriptures tell us that first He comes to gather His bride (the Church); then He returns with His Church (Rev. 19) for the final judgment. Our Lord said, "Watch therefore, for you know neither the day nor the hour in which the Son of Man is coming" (Matt. 25:13 NKJV).

If He were to come today, would we be ready? In the book of Daniel, our Lord has given us divine insight to His Word. As stated by Christ in Matthew 5:18,"Till heaven and earth pass, one jot or one tittle shall in no wise pass from the law, till all be fulfilled."

Christ has stated that His Word will come to pass. The Bible was written so we would not be ignorant of things to come. We are held accountable for what we know. What do you know or want to know? What will you do with God's only Son, Jesus Christ? Are you for Him or against Him?

Because our God is a loving God, He does not want any to perish but for all to come to repentance and accept His Son who died on the cross (2 Pet. 3:9). Our Lord is a gentleman! He will never force His way upon you, but He will be there to accept you with open arms.

God promises that He will keep born-again Christians from this great tribulation that will come upon the earth. "Because thou hast kept the word of my patience, I also will keep thee from the hour of temptation, which shall come upon all the world, to try them that dwell upon the earth" (Rev. 3:10).

Jesus promised eternal life for those who accept Him and follow Him. Again, you are invited to become a child of God; ask Him to come into your life; admit you are a sinner; repent of your sins; and follow Christ. Remember, the Lord knows your heart and when you accept Him He will fill you with His Holy Spirit, who will guide you and provide for you.

May the peace and grace of our Lord and Savior Jesus Christ reside in your hearts.

Chapter 10:
The Divine Outline

An Overview of the book of Revelation

The Holy Bible is a fascinating collection of sixty-six books inspired by God, written by forty authors. It is truly a collection of wisdom, guidance, knowledge, love, compassion, prophecy and inspiration. The Bible is a book that tells the beginning, the end and all the things in between. We start in Genesis (the Hebrew word for "Genesis" is Bereshith and means "in the beginning") and end in the book of Revelation. The book of Revelation was originally given the Greek name Apokalypsis Ioanno, which means "revelation of John." It is also known as Apokalypsis (Apocalypse), which means "the unveiling." However, the first verse of Revelation gives us the most accurate version of the theme of the book: Apokalypsis Iesou Christou, which means "the revelation of Jesus Christ, which God gave him [Jesus] to show his servants [John] the things which must happen soon" (Rev. 1:1 WEB).

To start this study, let's simplify the book by presenting it in three ways. The first is called The Divine Outline, which simplifies the book in a near-chronological view (other than a few places where we get a glimpse of heavenly scenes as well as chapter reviews). Next will be a chapter by chapter overview. The third presentation will parallel other books of the Bible with the book of Revelation so you will have a better understanding of the text.

First, though, I would like to share my first experience with the Bible. In 1976 as a fourteen-year-old junior high school student, I was given my first Bible at a party. The girl who gave me this blue denim Bible told me to read the book of Revelation! The next day I read the complete book of Revelation and was terrified. I thought to myself, What terror! How could a God of love pour out such wrath? So based on my experience, I have complete sympathy for anyone who reads Revelation and has a similar experience. Now, let's begin our study.

First, Revelation is the only book in the Bible that promises the reader a blessing. Revelation 1:3 says, "Blessed is he who reads and those who hear the words of the prophecy, and keep the things that are written in it, for the time is at hand" (WEB).

As you begin your study, you receive a blessing as well as inside knowledge on the importance of hearing, knowing and keeping the words of this prophecy. Therefore, as Christians, we need to understand this book and acknowledge what the Lord is asking us to do, which is to keep His Word. After all, Christ states repeatedly throughout Revelation, "He who has an ear, let him hear." Also, this is the last book of the Bible, and as with any book, the author trusts that you have read the entire book and comprehend the text or storyline. Let's elaborate more on the book by taking a look first at The Divine Outline.

John was sent to the island of Patmos, which is located about 100 miles southwest of Ephesus, where he received the word and then wrote the book of Revelation. Revelation 1:10–11 says, "I was in the Spirit on the Lord's day, and I heard behind me a loud voice, as of a trumpet, saying, "What you see, write in a book and send to the seven assemblies" (WEB).

John was then instructed, "Write therefore the things which you have seen, and the things which are, and the things which will happen hereafter" (Rev. 1:19 WEB).

Christ has now separated this book into three sections:

1. Write the things that you have seen: John saw Christ in His glory walking amid the churches.

   "And amid the lampstands [which represent the churches] was one like a son of man, clothed with a robe reaching down to his feet, and with a golden sash around his chest. His head and his hair were white as white wool, like snow. His feet were like burnished brass, as if it had been refined in a furnace. His voice was like the voice of many waters. He had seven stars in his right hand. Out of his mouth proceeded a sharp two-edged sword. His face was like the sun shining at its brightest (Rev. 1:13–16 WEB).

2. Write the things that are: This refers to the Church age or Church history, which is described in Revelation 2–3.
3. Write the things that will take place: This refers to the things that will happen after the Church age, which are presented in Revelation 4–22.

To simplify the book even more and to follow The Divine Outline of the book:

1. Chapter 1: John, after being given the vision, is instructed to write what he has seen
2. Chapters 2 and 3: Church history (starting with Pentecost to the twenty-first century)
3. Chapters 4 and 5: The Rapture of the Church and praising in heaven
4. ChapHeaven: The new world leader (or Antichrist) riding on a white horse

156

5. Chapters 6 to 18: The tribulation period (chapters 12 to 14 are reviews of previous events)
6. Chapter 19: Christ returns with His Church
7. Chapter 20: The millennium reign of Christ on earth, Satan bound, and the final judgment
8. Chapters 21 and 22: New heavens and new earth, promises of Christ coming

Now that you have a simplified overview of the book, let's elaborate chapter by chapter.

Chapter One

> This is the Revelation of Jesus Christ, which God gave him to show to his servants the things which must happen soon, which he sent and made known by his angel to his servant, John, who testified to God's word, and of the testimony of Jesus Christ, about everything that he saw. Blessed is he who reads and those who hear the words of the prophecy, and keep the things that are written in it, for the time is at hand. John, to the seven assemblies that are in Asia: Grace to you and peace, from God, who is and who was and who is to come; and from the seven Spirits who are before his throne; and from Jesus Christ, the faithful witness, the firstborn of the dead, and the ruler of the kings of the earth. To him who loves us, and washed us from our sins by his blood; and he made us to be a kingdom, priests to his God and Father; to him be the glory and the dominion forever and ever. Amen. Behold, he is coming with the clouds, and every eye will see him including those who pierced him. All the tribes of the earth will mourn over him. Even so, Amen. "I am the Alpha and the Omega, the Beginning and the End," says the Lord God, "who is and who was and who is to come, the Almighty." I John, your brother and partake,r with you in oppression and kingdom and perseverance which are in Jesus, was on the isle that is

called Patmos because of God's Word and the testimony of Jesus Christ. I was in the Spirit on the Lord's Day, and I heard behind me a loud voice, as of a trumpet saying, "What you see, write in a book and send to the seven assemblies: to Ephesus, Smyrna, Pergamum, Thyatira, Sardis, Philadelphia, and Laodicea." I turned to see the voice that spoke with me. When turned, I saw seven golden lampstands. And in the midsamidands was one like a son of man, clothed with a robe reaching down to his feet, and with a golden sash around his chest. His head and his hair were white as white wool, like snow. His eyes were like a flame of fire. His feet were like burnished brass, as if it had been refined in a furnace. His voice was like the voice of many waters. He had seven stars in his right hand. Out of his mouth proceeded a sharp two-edged sword. His face was like the sun shining at its brightest. When I saw him, I fell at his feet like a dead man. He laid his right hand on me, saying, "Don't be afraid. I am the first and the last, and the Living one. I was dead, and behold, I am alive forevermore. I have the keys of Death and of Hades. Write therefore the things which you have seen, and the things which are, and the things which will happen hereafter; the mystery of the seven stars which you saw in my right hand, and the seven golden lampstands. The seven stars are the angels of the seven assemblies. The seven lampstands are seven assemblies.

Chapter 1 set the scene. John was divinely instructed to write this glorious book that foretells the future. We read in that Christ is the faithful witness to God, just as we Christians are the faithful witness to Christ. He is the first begotten of the dead, the first to appear in a glorified body. He is the Prince of kings and rules over the kings of the earth. He has glory and dominion forever. In verse 7, there is a reminder of Christ's Second Coming: "Behold, he is coming with the clouds, and every eye will see him, including those who pierced him. All the tribes of the earth will mourn over him. Even so, Amen" (WEB). We also notice that Christ is always walking in the midst of the churches.

Chapter Two

> To the angel of the assembly in Ephesus write: "He who holds the seven stars in his right hand, he who walks in the midst of the seamidstands says these things: "I know your works, and your toil and perseverance, and that you can't tolerate evil men, and have tested those who call themselves apostles, and they are not, and found them false. You have perseverance and have endured for my name's sake, and have not grown weary. But I have this against you, that you left your first love. Remember therefore from where you have fallen, and repent and do the first works; or else I am coming to you, and will move your lampstand out of its place, unless you repent. But this you have, that you hate the works of the Nicolaitans, which I also hate. He who has an ear, let him hear what the Spirit says to the assemblies. To him who overcomes I will give to eat of the tree of life, which is in the Paradise of my God. To the angel of the assembly in Smyrna write: "The first and the last, who was dead, and has come to life says these things: "I know your oppression, and your poverty (but you are rich), and the blasphemy of those who say they are Jews, and they are not, but are a synagogue of Satan. Don't be afraid of the things which you are about to suffer. Behold, the devil is about to throw some of you into prison, that you may be tested; and you will have oppression for ten days. Be faithful to death, and I will give you the crown of life. He who has an ear, let him hear what the Spirit says to the assemblies. He who overcomes won't be hurt by the second death. To the angel of the assembly in Pergamum write: "He who has the sharp two-edged sword says

these things: "I know your works and where you dwell, where Satan's throne is. You hold firmly to my name, and didn't deny my faith, even in the days of Antipas my witness, my faithful one, who was killed among you, where Satan dwells. But I have a few things against you, because you have there some who hold the teaching of Balaam, who taught Balak to throw a stumbling block before the children of Israel, to eat things sacrificed to idols, and to commit sexual immorality. So you also have some who hold to the teaching of the Nicolaitans in the same way. Repent therefore, or else I am coming to you quickly, and I will make war against them with the sword of my mouth. He who has an ear, let him hear what the Spirit says to the assemblies. To him who overcomes, to him will I give of the hidden manna, and I will give him a white stone, and on the stone a new name written, which no one knows but he is writtenceives it.*

To the angel of the assembly in Thyatira write: "The Son of God, who has his eyes like a flame of fire, and his feet are like burnished brass, says these things: I know your works, your love, faith, service, patient endurance, and that your last works are more than the first. But I have this against you, that you tolerate your woman, Jezebel, who calls herself a prophetess. She teaches and seduces my servants to commit sexual immorality, and to eat things sacrificed to idols. I gave her time to repent, but she refuses to repent of her sexual immorality. Behold, I will throw her into a bed, and those who commit adultery with her into great oppression, unless they repent of her works. I will kill her children with Death, and all the assemblies will know that I am he who searches the minds and hearts. I will give to each one of you according to your deeds. But to you I say, to the rest who are in Thyatira, as many as don't have this teaching, who don't know what some call 'the deep things of Satan,' to you I say, I don't lay on you any other burden. Nevertheless that which you have, hold firmly until I come. He who overcomes, and he who keeps my works to the end, to him will I give authority over the nations. He will rule them with a rod of iron, shattering them like clay pots; as I also have received of my Father: and I will give him the morning star. He who has an ear, let him hear what the Spirit says to the assemblies (Rev. 2 WEB).

It is amazing that the Holy Spirit laid out the seven churches in chronological order. The book of Acts covers the first thirty years of the church, while Revelation 2–3 covers church history thereafter until the present day. This fills the gap between Daniel's sixty-ninth and seventieth week. Now, if you take a moment and think about the churches that are listed, it makes you wonder why He mentioned these seven and not Jerusalem, Colossae, Galatia or Antioch.

Let's take a look at what the seven churches represent historically and presently:

1. Ephesus: *Apostolic Age (Pentecost-100 A.D.)*
2. Smyrna: *Age of Persecution (100–313)*
3. Pergamos: *State Religion Church (313–590)*
4. Thyatira: *Age of Papacy/Catholicism (590–present)*
5. Sardis: *Reformation/Protestant (1517–present)*
6. Philadelphia: *Missionary Church (1730–Rapture)*
7. Laodicea: *Apostate Church (19th century–present)*

Note that the last four churches are present-day churches.

Ephesus was the city where John lived; it was a great cosmopolitan society and a major harbor for Asia (modern-day Turkey). Ephesus was located on the east side of the Aegean Sea along the southwest coast of Asia. That would be its historical relevance. Christ complimented the church of Ephesus on their labors, their patience and the fact that they could not bear evil. They were also tested and had discernment; they were not easily misled, and they hated the deeds of the Nicolaitans (the establishing of priesthood) which Christ also hates. Yet, Christ rebuked them for leaving their first love. They had all of the motions of a good church, yet they did not have the emotions (love of God). Christ then said, "Remember therefore from where you have fallen, and repent and do the first works" (Rev. 2:5 WEB). In other words, Christ was saying, "At first you loved Me, and then you got caught up in works and religion and lost sight of Me." A good example of this is Mary and Martha. When Christ came over for dinner, Mary sat at Christ's feet and listened, while Martha was worried about worldly things. Christ pointed this out to Martha (Luke 10:40–42). Also, please note that the church of Ephesus was within the first 100 years of church history, and they had already lost their first love. Ephesus was the loveless church.

Smyrna was located thirty-five miles north of Ephesus at the head of a gulf, which made the city a good port and an important trade center. Smyrna was an educational center and had fine schools for medicine and science. (Today it is the city of Izmir in Turkey.) Smyrna was known as the persecuted church and was ended in about AD 313 by Constantine. It is estimated that about 5 million Christians were martyred under the rule of the Roman government during the period of persecution. (Read Fox's Book of Martyrs for more precise details.) Christ commended the church of Smyrna; He identified Himself as formerly dead but now alive, in order to give them hope that they too would live (that they would have the hope of the resurrection). He knew their works, tribulation and poverty. He said that they were rich and that He knew the blasphemy of those who said they were Jews (or Israel governed by God) yet were from the synagogues of Satan. At that time, the Jews hated the Gentiles, and Christ stated that if the Jews were truly governed by God, then they would not act with hatred. He also forewarns the church that they would be persecuted (or have tribulation) for ten days. The ten days allude to the ten Roman emperors who supported persecution:

1. Nero
2. Domitian
3. Trajan
4. Hadrian
5. Septimius Severus
6. Maximin
7. Decius
8. Valerian
9. Aurelian
10. Diocletian

The interesting thing about the church of Smyrna is that Christ did not say anything bad about it. In fact, He said, "I will give you the crown of life. He who overcomes won't be hurt by the second death" (Rev 2:10–11 WEB).

For those who are not born again there are two deaths; if you are "born twice" you will die only once (unless you are taken in the Rapture).

Pergamos (modern-day Bergama) was a city located fifty miles north of Smyrna, about fifteen miles from the sea. The city itself was known as the religious center of the province of Asia. It was a luxurious city, yet it was filled with demonic powers. It was also noted for its fine library, and it was a place where parchments were first used. In Pergamum, four temples were erected in honor of the cults (Zeus, Athena, Dionysus and Asclerius). The church of Pergamos represents the first state religion.

Constantine developed a system whereby the world became part of the church. This church was in the midst of Satan's throne—among temples and demonic worship—yet they held fast to Christ's name. However, Pergamos was a compromising church that allowed idolatry. Christ said, "You have there some who hold the teaching of Balaam, who taught Balak to throw a stumbling block before the children of Israel" (Rev. 2:14 WEB). The church was compromising by worshipping relics. Christ also scolded them for holding the doctrine of the Nicolaitans (the priesthood), which He hated. Christ then went on to say, "Repent therefore, or else I am coming to you quickly, and I will make war against them with the sword of my mouth. He who has an ear, let him hear what the Spirit says to the assemblies" (Rev. 2:16–17 WEB).

Thyatira (modern-day Akhisar) was located forty miles southeast of Pergamum. Thyatira was known for its manufacturing (garments, pottery, brass, etc.). It was also the city of the temple dedicated to Tyrimnos, an ancient-day sun god. Christ said, "I know your works, your love, faith, service, patient endurance, and that your last works are more than the first" (Rev. 2:19 WEB).

Christ was saying that the church focused more on good works than on love. Christ then added, "Nevertheless I have a few things against you, because you allow that woman Jezebel, who calls herself a prophetess, to teach and seduce My servants to commit sexual immorality and eat things sacrificed to idols" (Rev. 2:20 NKJV). If you remember the story of Jezebel, she brought idols, such as Baal, into Israel for help and guidance. This is spiritual idolatry. We need be totally committed to Jesus; commitment to anything before the Lord is a sin. God said to the children of Israel,

> *Thou shalt have no other gods before me. Thou shalt not make unto thee any graven image, or any likeness of anything that is in heaven above, or that is in the earth beneath, or that is in the water under the earth. Thou shalt not bow down thyself to them, nor serve them (Ex. 20:3–5).*

Christ then said to the church, "Behold, I will throw her into a bed, and those who commit adultery with her into great oppression, unless they repent of her works" (Rev 2:22 WEB).

We can see from the text that this church is a modern day church, and if they repent, they will be kept from the great tribulation. Thyatira represents today's Roman Catholic religion and is referred to as the corrupt church.

Chapter Three

> And to the angel of the assembly in Sardis write: He who has the seven Spirits of God, and the seven stars says these things: "I know your works that you have a reputation of being alive, but you are dead. Wake up, and establish the things that remain, which were ready to die, for I have found no works of yours perfected before my God. Remember therefore how you have received and heard. Keep it, and repent. If therefore you won't watch, I will come as a thief, and you won't know what hour I will come on you. Nevertheless you have a few names in Sardis that did not defile their garments. They will walk with me in white, for they are worthy. He who overcomes will be arrayed like this in white garments, and I will in no way blot his name out of the book of life, and I will confess his name before my Father, and before his angels. He who has an ear, let him hear what the Spirit says to the assemblies. To the angel of the assembly in Philadelphia write: "He who is holy, he who is true, he who has the key of David, he who opens and no one can shut, and that shuts and no one opens, says these things: "I know your works (behold, I have set before you an open door, which no one can shut), that you have a little power, and kept my word, and didn't deny my name. Behold, I give of the synagogue of Satan, of those who say they are Jews, and they are not, but lie. Behold, I will make them to come and worship before

your feet, and to know that I have loved you. Because you kept the word of my patience, I also will keep you from the hour of testing, that which is to come on the whole world, to test those who dwell on the earth. I come quickly. Hold firmly that which you have, so that no one takes your crown. He who overcomes, I will make him a pillar in the temple of my God, and he will go out from there no more. I will write on him the name of my God, and the name of the city of my God, the New Jerusalem, which comes down out of heaven from my God, and my own new name. He who has an ear, let him hear what the Spirit says to the assemblies. To the angel of the assembly in Laodicea write: "The Amen, the Faithful and True Witness, the Head of God's creation, says these things: "I know your works, that you are neither cold nor hot. I wish you were cold or hot. So, because you are lukewarm, and neither hot nor cold, I will vomit you out of my mouth. Because you say, 'I am rich, and have gotten riches, and have need of nothing;' and don't know that you are the wretched one, miserable, poor, blind, and naked; I counsel you to buy from me gold refined by fire, that you may become rich; and white garments, that you may clothe yourself, and that the shame of your nakedness may not be revealed; and eye salve to anoint your eyes, that you may see. As many as I love, I reprove and chasten. Be zealous therefore, and repent. Behold, I stand at the door and knock. If anyone hears my voice and opens the door, I will come in to him, and will dine with him, and he with me. He who overcomes, I will give to him to sit down with me on my throne, as I also overcame, and sat down with my Father on his throne. He who has an ear, let him hear what the Spirit says to the assemblies" (Rev. 3 WEB).

Sardis was located about thirty miles southeast of Thyatira. The ancient city stood on the northern slopes of a mountain with a river flowing at its base. It was a very wealthy city and considered militarily impregnable. Sardis was also known for its pagan worship of Sybele, a goddess similar to Diana in Ephesus. Christ said to the church of Sardis, "I know your works, which you have a reputation of being alive, but you are dead" (Rev. 3:1 WEB).

This comment refers to the Protestant Reformation. The church had the right idea, but they still followed Babylonian traditions. The principles of the Reformation were correct, but they taught infant baptism, which teaches works rather than being born again. Other dominations came out of the Reformation. In Revelation 3:3, Christ said to the church, "Remember therefore how you have received and heard. Keep it, and repent. If therefore you won't watch, I will come as a thief, and you won't know what hour I will come on you" (WEB). Christ was telling the church to go back to its roots and to be ready for His return, to remember their origins. The just shall live by faith (Romans 1:17) and by the power of the Spirit. Do not get caught up in denominations and religiosity. Go back to God's Word, for He is coming quickly.

> "He who overcomes will be arrayed like this in white garments, and I will in no way blot his name out of the book of life, and I will confess his name before my Father, and before his angels. He who has an ear, let him hear what the Spirit says to the assemblies" (Rev. 3:5–6 WEB).

Sardis was known as the *dead church*.

Philadelphia, located twenty-eight miles southwest of Sardis, was a wealthy trade center, situated on a terrace above the banks of the Cogamus River. Philadelphia was known as "Little Athens" because of its magnificent temples and public buildings. The word Philadelphia comes from the Greek word Philo and means "the city of brotherly love." Christ said to the church of Philadelphia, "I know your works (behold, I have set before you an open door, which no one can shut), that you have a little power, and kept my word, and didn't deny my name" (Rev. 3:8 WEB).

First, notice that Christ opened doors for this church that no one can shut. Next, notice that this is a Bible-teaching church; Christ stated that they kept His Word, and He commended them because they did not deny His name. This is referring to the "born-again" church. Christ then added, "Because you have kept My command [a command, not a suggestion] to persevere, I also will keep you from the hour of trial [or tribulation] which shall come upon the whole world, to test those who dwell on the earth" (Rev. 3:10 NKJV). Christ is referring to the Rapture of the church here. He states that He will keep them from the tribulation, which the whole world will endure.

Note: the outline that has been prepared does not spend a lot of time dealing with the trials and tribulation in Revelation 6–18, mainly because as "born-again Christians" we will not be here to experience this tribulation. Therefore, the focus is primarily on the glorious time with the Father in heaven rather than on the wrath or the tribulation on the earth. It is valid to explain in brief what the world will experience to encourage readers to give their lives to the Lord so that they may bypass this tribulation period promised to the non-believers.

Christ tells us, "Hold fast what you have, that no one may take your crown" (Rev. 3:11 NKJV).

> "He who overcomes, I will make him a pillar in the temple of my God, and he will go out from there no more. I will write on him the name of my God, and the name of the city of my God, the New Jerusalem, which comes down out of heaven from my God, and my own new

name. He who has an ear, let him hear what the Spirit says to the assemblies" (Rev. 3:12–13 WEB).

How many of you have ears? Christ is telling you to listen to what He is saying. Smyrna and Philadelphia were listening, the only two churches that were not criticized by Christ.

Laodicea was located in the Lycus valley on a major crossroads forty-five miles southeast of Philadelphia, about ninety miles east of Ephesus. Laodicea was an extremely prosperous banking and commercial center (perhaps the modern-day Wall Street). The city was also popular for its medical studies and manufacturing of clothing. Christ said to the church of Laodicea, "I know your works, that you are neither cold nor hot. I wish you were cold or hot. So, because you are lukewarm, and neither hot nor cold, I will vomit you out of my mouth" (Rev. 3:15–16 WEB).

Christ told the church that they made Him sick. They knew the Word but were not living the Word. It would've been better for them to not know Christ than to pretend to know Christ and not heed His commands. Christ went on to say,

> *"Because you say, 'I am rich, have become wealthy, and have need of nothing'—and do not know that you are wretched, miserable, poor, blind, and naked—I counsel you to buy from Me gold refined in the fire, that you may be rich; and white garments, that you may be clothed, that the shame of your nakedness may not be revealed; and anoint your eyes with eye salve, that you may see" (Rev. 3:17–18 NKJV).*

Take note, this church is the big fundraising church; they have the big production, yet they are working for themselves, not for the Lord. Christ told them to take their riches and give them up for true salvation, to come to Him and be clothed in white, to be made pure and to have their eyes opened. This church was a for-profit ministry and did not seek the kingdom of our Lord. That is why in the next verse Christ said, "As many as I love, I rebuke and chasten. Therefore be zealous and repent" (Rev. 3:19 NKJV). In other words, "You are profiting through the power of Satan, and if you do not repent, you may have all the things of this world but will lose your eternity in heaven."

It is interesting that Christ then quoted, "Behold, I stand at the door and knock. If anyone hears My voice and opens the door, I will come in to him and dine with him, and he with Me" (Rev. 3:20 NKJV). There are two things that are very interesting about this statement. The first is that Christ told the church that He was standing outside the door and knocking at their hearts, yet the church would not let Him in. Our Lord is a gentleman; He will never force His way in. He will lovingly and patently be there waiting for us to respond. Next, we should note that Christ wants to dine with us! To understand the intimacy of this statement, you need to understand the culture of those days (which is the same as Middle Eastern culture today). It was not about fast food and drive-through; to dine with someone was to let them into your house and dip bread in bowls of oils and spices with you. (That is why in Jewish law it was unclean to let a Gentile into a Jewish house.) It was a sit-on-pillows-on-the-floor-and-relax relationship. Christ is saying, "Let Me in so that we can be intimate with each other; let Me get to know you and you Me." Christ wants to have that kind of relationship with His brethren. He wants to be part of our lives. In conclusion, Christ says, "To him who overcomes I will grant to sit with Me on My throne…He who has an ear, let him hear what the Spirit says to the churches" (Rev. 3:21–22 NKJV).

Laodicea is known as the apostate church.

Chapter Four

After these things I looked and saw a door opened in heaven, and the first voice that I heard, like a trumpet speaking with me, was one saying, "Come up here, and I will show you the things which must happen after this." Immediately I was in the Spirit. Behold, there was a throne set in heaven, and one sitting on the throne that looked like a jasper stone and a sardius. There was a rainbow around the throne, like an emerald to look at. Around the throne were twenty-four thrones. On the thrones were twenty-four elders sitting, dressed in white garments, with crowns of gold on their heads. Out of the throne proceed lightnings, sounds, and thunders. There were seven lamps of fire burning before the throne, which are the seven Spirits of God. Before the throne was something like a sea of glass, like a crystal. In the midst of the throne, and around the throne were four living creatures full of eyes before and behind. The first creature was like a lion, and the second creature like a calf, and the third creature had a face like a man, and the fourth creature was like a flying eagle. And the four living creatures, having each one of them six wings, are full of eyes around about and within. They have no rest day and night, saying, Holy, holy, holy is the Lord God, the Almighty, who was and who is and who is to come. When the living creatures give glory, honor, and thanks to him who sits on the throne, to him who lives forever and ever, the twenty-four elders fall down before him who sits on the throne, and worship him who lives forever and ever, and will throw their crowns before the throne, saying, "Worthy are you, our Lord and our God, to receive the glory, the honor, and the power, for you created all things, and because of your desire they existed, and were created" (Rev. 4 WEB).

This chapter starts out with the Greek word meta-tauta (met-ah'tow-tah), which, in its context literally means "after these things." You might ask yourself, "After what things?" The answer is, after the church. John's spirit was lifted into heaven, and there he saw the throne of God. (Scholars feel this is the time the Rapture of the church takes place.) Second Thessalonians 2:6-7 tells us that the Holy Spirit will continue to restrain the Antichrist until it is removed. The hindering force is the Holy Spirit within the believers. Once the believers are raptured, the world leader will come into power.) John saw God on His throne in all of His splendor and glory. Around the throne sat twenty-four elders. (Some Bible scholars believe that the twenty-four elders could represent the twelve tribes of Israel and the twelve apostles.) We then read of four living creatures, which are heavenly beings (thought to be cherubims). Chapter 4 represents the vision of God, the creator of all things, sitting on His heavenly throne, whereas in chapter 5 Christ is presented as the redeemer, the Lion of the tribe of Judah and the Root of David who has prevailed to open the scroll. (Note that some translations say "book," yet in the Greek, the word means "scroll.")

Chapter Five

> I saw, in the right hand of him who sat on the throne, a book written within and on the back, sealed shut with seven seals. I saw a mighty angel proclaiming with a loud voice, "Who is worthy to open the book, and to break its seals?" No one in heaven, or on the earth, or under the earth, was able to open the book, or to look in it. And I wept much, because no one was found worthy to open the book, or to look in it. One of the elders said to me, "Don't weep. Behold, the Lion who is of the tribe of Judah, the Root of David, has overcome to open the book and its seven seals." I saw in the midst of the throne and of the four living creatures, and in the midst of the elders, a Lamb standing, as though it had been slain,

having seven horns, and seven eyes, which are the seven Spirits of God, sent forth into all the earth. Then he came, and he took it out of the right hand of him who sat on the throne. Now when he had taken the book, the four living creatures and the twenty-four elders fell down before the Lamb, each one having a harp, and golden bowls full of incense, which are the prayers of the saints. They sang a new song, saying, "You are worthy to take the book, And to open its seals: For you were killed, And bought us for God with your blood, Out of every tribe, language, people, and nation, And made them kings and priests to our God, And they reign on earth." I saw, and I heard a voice of many angels around the throne, the living creatures, and the elders; and the number of them was ten thousands of ten thousands, and thousands of thousands; saying with a loud voice, "Worthy is the Lamb who has been killed to receive the power, riches, wisdom, might, honor, glory, and blessing!" I heard every created thing which is in heaven, on the earth, under the earth, on the sea, and everything in them, saying, "To him who sits on the throne, and to the Lamb be the blessing, the honor, the glory, and the dominion, forever and ever. Amen." The four living creatures said, "Amen!" The elders fell down and worshiped (Rev. 5 WEB).

The scroll represents the title deed to the earth. If this sounds strange to you, perhaps we should take a quick course, Jewish Culture and Law 101, for a better understanding of the text. However, before doing so, we need to review what happened in Genesis that brought about the fall of man. In Genesis 2:17, man was told, "But you must not eat from the tree of the knowledge of good and evil, for when you eat of it you will surely die" (NIV). In disobeying, man's flesh died in this world and was separated from God. This episode also caused the earth to be given to Satan, who was given power over it. And if you recall, in the Gospels Christ was tempted by Satan, and Satan offered Christ all the splendors of this world. It is interesting that Christ never denied the fact that Satan could offer and fulfill all these earthly things. The fact is, Christ died for our sins and paid the price to redeem us, yet He has not yet taken possession of the earth. (Romans 11:25 tells us that God is waiting for the fullness of the Gentiles to come in before He returns for His Church.) So as of today, Satan has control of this world and will continue to have control until Christ loosens the seal of the title deed of the earth.

Now let's take that course in Jewish Culture and Law 101. If a person lost his land, he then had the right to purchase it back after a set amount of time. This law was established so that the Israelites would not lose their inheritance. If the original owner could not fulfill the requirements to purchase back the land, then a family member or next of kin could do so for him. This law was established to keep the inheritance in the possession of the original tribe that God had allocated the land to.

If you were to forfeit your land (usually because of financial circumstances), the new owner would take the deed to the property and write down on a scroll the fee or requirement for you to purchase the land back. The scroll would then be sealed shut. At the end of the given time, if the owner could not meet the requirements in order to purchase back his land but a family member or next of kin could, then that family member could redeem the land for the family. This person was called the kinsmen redeemer, or in Hebrew the goel. It is also very interesting that this transaction had to take place at the city gates in front of the elders and the authorities. (To read about this practice in depth, read the book of Ruth.)

In Revelation 5:7, we have Christ, our Kinsmen Redeemer, stepping up to receive the scroll from the Father's right hand (the right hand always signifies power). Christ appears as a

Lamb that was slain, who has paid the price in full and is now ready to claim the title deed to the earth. Picture this, if you would: Christ is described as the Lion of the tribe of Judah but also as the Lamb that was slain. The Lion represents Christ as the conqueror over Satan, whereas the Lamb satisfies the justice of God. His marks identify His suffering as He interceded for our sins and brought us redemption through His blood. What a glorious sight! There is continual praise and worship in heaven, and all will sing praises to the Lord in heaven, words that only the redeemed church can sing (Rev. 5:9–10). And all will enjoy the marriage supper of the Lamb and spend seven glorious years worshipping in heaven with our Lord. Christ comes forward to take authority over what is rightfully His. This is where we receive the long-awaited answers to our prayer: "Thy kingdom come, Thy will be done in earth" (Matt. 6:10).

Chapter Six

I saw that the Lamb opened one of the seven seals, and I heard one of the four living creatures saying, as with a voice of thunder, "Come and see!" I saw, and behold, a white horse, and he who sat on it had a bow. A crown was given to him, and he came forth conquering, and to conquer. When he opened the second seal, I heard the second living creature saying, "Come!" Another came forth, a red horse. To him who sat on it was given to take peace from the earth, and that they should kill one another. There was given to him a great sword. When he opened the third seal, I heard the third living creature saying, "Come and see!" I saw, and behold, a black horse. He who sat on it had a balance in his hand. I heard a voice in the midst of the four living creatures saying, "A choenix of wheat for a denarius, and three choenix of barley for a denarius! Don't damage the oil and the wine!" When he opened the fourth seal, I heard the voice of the fourth living creature saying, "Come and see!" I saw, and behold, a pale horse. He who sat on him, his name was Death. Hades followed with him. Authority over one fourth of the earth, to kill with the sword, with famine, with death, and by the wild animals of the earth was given to them. When he opened the fifth seal, I saw underneath the altar the souls of those who had been killed for the word of God, and for the testimony which they held. They cried with a loud voice, saying, "How long, Master, the holy and true, do you not judge and avenge our blood on those who dwell on the earth?" There was given to each one of them a white robe. It was said to them that they should rest yet for a little time, until their fellow servants and their brothers, who would also be killed even as they were, had been fulfilled. I saw when he opened the sixth seal, and there was a great earthquake. The sun became black as sackcloth made of hair, and the whole moon became as blood. The stars of the sky fell to the earth, as a fig tree drops its unripe figs when it is shaken by a great wind. The sky was removed as a scroll when it is rolled up. Every mountain and island were moved out of their places. The kings of the earth, the princes, the commanding officers, the rich, the strong, and every slave and freeman, hid themselves in the caves and in the rocks of the mountains. They told the mountains and the rocks, "Fall on us, and hide us from the face of him who sits on the throne, and from the wrath of the Lamb, for the great day of his wrath has come; and who is able to stand?" (Rev. 6 WEB).

It begins with the opening of the first seal and the rider on the white horse, the new world leader (Antichrist). In other words, this world leader will bring about his own empire or kingdom. He is to be a charismatic man who will win the world over with his charm and his excellent good business skills. He will appear as the man with all the answers, yet after three and-a-half years, he will unveil his true nature (Dan. 9:27).

Next comes the rider of the red horse, the second seal (Rev. 6:4). This horse represents war. Following is the third horseman, who brings in famine, and as history shows us, famine always follows war. In this day and age, a nuclear war would contaminate the soil for many years to come, and this would make for world-wide famine. Also, people will have to pay exorbitant prices for a meal—if one is available. A quart of wheat will cost a denarius (a whole day's pay). Finally, the fourth horseman pours out his wrath (Rev. 6:8). This pale horse brings about disease, more hunger, and death to a fourth of the earth—approximately 1 billion people.

Verses 9 and 10 usher in the breaking of the fifth seal, revealing underneath the altar, the cry of the martyrs. These are the people who were not caught up in the Rapture. During the time of tribulation they put their trust in Christ and are martyred for their faith (Rev. 6:9–10). Then seal number six is opened (Rev: 6:12–13), and a great earthquake with cataclysmic disasters occur. "For the great day of His wrath has come, and who is able to stand?" (Rev. 6:17 NKJV).

Chapter Seven

> *After this, I saw four angels standing at the four corners of the earth, holding the four winds of the earth, so that no wind would blow on the earth, or on the sea, or on any tree. I saw another angel ascend from the sunrise, having the seal of the living God. He cried with a loud voice to the four angels to whom it was given to harm the earth and the sea, saying, "Don't harm the earth, neither the sea, nor the trees, until we have sealed the bondservants of our God on their foreheads!" I heard the number of those who were sealed, one hundred forty-four thousand, sealed out of every tribe of the*

children of Israel: Of the tribe of Judah were sealed twelve thousand, Of the tribe of Reuben twelve thousand, Of the tribe of Gad twelve thousand, Of the tribe of Asher twelve thousand, Of the tribe of Naphtali twelve thousand, Of the tribe of Manasseh twelve thousand, Of the tribe of Simeon twelve thousand, Of the tribe of Levi twelve thousand, Of the tribe of Issachar twelve thousand, Of the tribe of Zebulun twelve thousand, Of the tribe of Joseph twelve thousand, Of the tribe of Benjamin were sealed twelve thousand. After these things I saw, and behold, a great multitude, which no man could number, out of every nation and of all tribes, peoples, and languages, standing before the throne and before the Lamb, dressed in white robes, with palm branches in their hands. They cried with a loud voice, saying, "Salvation be to our God, who sits on the throne, and to the Lamb." All the angels were standing around the throne, the elders, and the four living creatures; and they fell before the throne on their faces, and worshiped God, saying, "Amen! Blessing, glory, wisdom, thanksgiving, honor, power, and might, be to our God forever and ever! Amen." One of the elders answered, saying to me, "These who are arrayed in white robes, who are they, and where did they come from?" I told him, "My lord, you know." He said to me, "These are those who came out of the great oppression. They washed their robes, and made them white in the Lamb's blood. Therefore are they before the throne of God, they serve him day and night in his temple. He who sits on the throne will spread his tent over them. They will never be hungry, neither thirsty anymore; neither will the sun beat on them, nor any heat; for the Lamb who is in the midst of the throne will be their shepherd, and will guide them to living springs of waters. God will wipe away every tear from their eyes" (Rev. 7 WEB).

Revelation 7 introduces the 144,000 Jews who will be protected through the tribulation period. There are 12,000 from the twelve tribes of Israel. In verses 9 to 15, we have a great multitude of all nations (greater than ever seen) before the throne of God. We are told in verse 14 that these are the ones who came out of the great tribulation and washed their robes clean in His blood. These are the people who gave their lives to the Lord during the tribulation and were martyred for their faith. We also notice in verse 15 that they serve God night and day. It is interesting that the raptured church is represented as the bride of Christ, whereas these tribulation saints become servants. I often hear Christians say, "If I miss the rapture, then I will commit my life to Christ during the tribulation!" Let me emphasize this: If you cannot live for Christ today, why do you assume that you can die for Him then?

However, the text does state that there will be more people who give their lives to the Lord during the tribulation period than are taken up in the Rapture. (I believe that many of these will be people who heard the Scriptures presented but never walked with the Lord or accepted His invitation. Perhaps these tribulation-saints recall hearing about an event of this kind happening. This prompts them to study the Scriptures, which leads them into making a profession of faith and following Christ. And for this, they are martyred.)

As discussed earlier, the purpose of this outline is not to emphasize the destruction being foretold but to encourage the believer that whoever follows the Lord will be kept from this wrath, which is promised to fall upon the whole earth. And because it is written, it is appropriate for the sake of the non-believers, as well as lukewarm Christians, to expound upon this tribulation period that is to come. Now let us take a look at chapter 8.

Chapter Eight

When he opened the seventh seal, there followed a silence in heaven for about half an hour. I saw the seven angels who stand before God, and seven trumpets were given to them. Another angel came and stood over the altar, having a golden censer. Much incense was given to him that he should add it to the prayers of all the saints on the golden altar which was before the throne. The smoke of the incense, with the prayers of the saints, went up before God out of the angel's hand. The angel took the censer, and he filled it with the fire of the altar, and threw it on the earth. There followed thunders, sounds, lightnings, and an earthquake. The seven angels who had the seven trumpets prepared themselves to sound. The first sounded, and there followed hail and fire, mixed with blood, and they were thrown on the earth. One third of the earth was burnt up, and one third of the trees were burnt up, and all green grass was burnt up. The second angel sounded, and something like a great mountain burning with fire was thrown into the sea. One third of the sea became blood, and one third of the creatures which were in the sea died, those who had life. One third of the ships were destroyed. The third angel sounded, and a great star fell from the sky, burning like a torch, and it fell on one third of the rivers, and on the springs of the waters. The name of the star is called "Wormwood." One third of the waters became wormwood. Many men died from the waters, because they were made bitter. The fourth angel sounded, and one third of the sun was struck, and one third of the moon, and one third of the stars; so that one third of them would be darkened, and the day wouldn't shine for one third of it, and the night in the same way. I saw, and I heard an eagle, flying in mid heaven, saying with a loud voice, "Woe! Woe! Woe for those who dwell on the earth, because of the other voices of the trumpets of the three angels, who are yet to sound" (Rev. 8 WEB).

An angel offering prayers to God starts off this chapter. The smoke of burning incense ascends from the golden altar. You may recall that the earthly altar was a replica of the altar in heaven, and the burning incense represents the prayers of the people that the priest would present to God. Now comes the opening of the seventh and last seal. Seven is God's perfect number, the number of completion (e.g., there are seven days in a week, seven notes in a musical scale, etc.). When this last seal is opened, the seven trumpets of the seven angels come out to sound. (The trump of God is different than the trumpet call of the angels.)

The first angel sounded (Rev. 8:7). This judgment seems to destroy parts of the earth's vegetation. The second trumpet sounded and destroyed one-third of the seas (Rev. 8:10–11). Plague destroyed one-third of the earth's drinking water. The fourth angel sounded his trumpet, and one-third of the sun, moon and stars were darkened. "Woe! Woe! Woe for those who dwell on the earth, because of the other voices of the trumpets of the three angels, who are yet to sound" (Rev. 8:13 WEB).

Just think: after the starvation, thirst, and darkness the angels proclaim, now is the time when "true" torment will come! What a terrifying thought! (Isn't it wonderful to already be under the grace of our Lord? He says in Revelation 3:10, "Because you have kept My command to persevere, I also will keep you from the hour of trial" (NKJV).

Chapter Nine

> *The fifth angel sounded, and I saw a star from the sky fallen to the earth. The key to the pit of the abyss was given to him. He opened the pit of the abyss, and smoke went up out of the pit, like the smoke from a great furnace. The sun and the air were darkened because of the smoke from the pit. Then out of the smoke came*

forth locusts on the earth, and power was given to them, as the scorpions of the earth have power. They were told that they should not hurt the grass of the earth, neither any green thing, neither any tree, but only those men who don't have God's seal on their foreheads. They were given power not to kill them, but to torment them for five months. Their torment was like the torment of a scorpion, when it strikes a man. In those days men will seek death, and will in no way find it. They will desire to die, and death will flee from them. The shapes of the locusts were like horses prepared for war. On their heads were something like gold crowns, and their faces were like men's faces. They had hair like women's hair, and their teeth were like those of lions. They had breastplates, like breastplates of iron. The sound of their wings was like the sound of chariots, or of many horses rushing to war. They have tails like those of scorpions, and stings. In their tails is their power to harm men for five months. They have over them as king the angel of the abyss. His name in Hebrew is "Abaddon," but in Greek, he has the name "Apollyon." The first woe is past. Behold, there are still two woes coming after this. The sixth angel sounded. I heard a voice from the horns of the golden altar which is before God, saying to the sixth angel who had one trumpet, "Free the four angels who are bound at the great river Euphrates." The four angels were freed who had been prepared for that hour and day and month and year, so that they would kill one third of mankind. The number of the armies of the horsemen was two hundred million. I heard the number of them. Thus I saw the horses in the vision, and those who sat on them, having breastplates of fiery red, hyacinth blue, and sulfur yellow; and the heads of lions. Out of their mouths proceed fire, smoke, and sulfur. By these three plagues were one third of mankind killed: by the fire, the smoke, and the sulfur, which proceeded out of their mouths. For the power of the horses is in their mouths, and in their tails. For their tails are like serpents, and have heads, and with them they harm. The rest of mankind, who were not killed with these plagues, didn't repent of the works of their hands, that they wouldn't worship demons, and the idols of gold, and of silver, and of brass, and of stone, and of wood; which can neither see, nor hear, nor walk. They didn't repent of their murders, nor of their sorceries, nor of their sexual immorality, nor of their thefts (Rev. 9 WEB).

As we enter chapter 9, we read, "Then the fifth angel sounded: And I saw a star fallen from heaven to the earth. To him was given the key to the bottomless pit" (Rev. 9:1 NKJV).

We know that a star from heaven refers here to an angel, which would be none other than Satan. This is where Satan is denied access to the throne of God. If this seems weird to you, you need to remember that up until this time, Satan had access to the throne of God. (For more detailed information on this topic, please read the book of Job.) Reading on, we are told that Satan is given the key to the bottomless pit. This now reveals what the angels meant in the previous chapter when they proclaimed "Woe for those who dwell on the earth" (Rev. 8:13 WEB).

At this time, Satan will release demonic spirits and demons upon the earth. We read of people who have intense suffering yet are not able to die. It's fascinating to note that these demonic spirits are commanded not to touch the 144,000 who are sealed by God. (Again, the book of Job will help you understand the dialogue between God and Satan and how God restricts Satan from certain things.) Verse 11 talks about the leader of these demons being a king. He is called the angel of the bottomless pit, whose name in the Hebrew is Abaddon, but in the Greek he is named Appollyon. Next, the sixth angel sounds his trumpet to release the four angels who were bound at the great Euphrates. These angels have been prepared for this hour, day and year. They will be released to kill one-third of mankind. These angels are fallen angels who did not keep their first state and were, therefore, chained in darkness and kept for this great day of Judgment (see Jude 1:6 for more details).

To "set the stage" for these events, think about these four demonic, powerful angels going out and causing destruction upon men. Could this be what our Lord was talking about when He said, "For then there will be great tribulation, such as has not been since the beginning of the world until this time, no, nor ever shall be" (Matt. 24:21 NKJV)?

An army of 200 million soldiers will march to battle, and together they will cause war. Their weapons, fire, smoke and brimstone will kill another one-third of mankind. In the days that John wrote this book, there were not even 200 million able-bodied fighting men on the face of the earth. Now, one nation alone (China) can house an army of 200 million fighting solders. The text also reads that from their heads and tails will come fire, smoke and brimstone that kills one-third of mankind! How could John describe today's sophisticated weapons nearly 2,000 years ago? Could this army John described be outfitted with tanks, missile launchers and other military weapons? In the days of John, swords, horses and flaming arrows were the weapons used for military battle.

We read in Revelation 9:21 that men still do not repent of their deeds, and they continue to worship their idols. They do not give up stealing, sexual immorality or sorcery. The word sorceries in the Greek is pharmakeia, which means "drugs." It is simply amazing that no matter how bad it gets, carnal mankind will not look up to Christ for salvation. Instead, they will curse Him for their miseries.

Chapter Ten

I saw another mighty angel coming down out of the sky, clothed with a cloud. A rainbow was on his head. His face was like the sun, and his feet like pillars of fire. He had in his hand a little book open. He set his right foot on the sea, and his left on the land. He cried with a loud voice, as a lion roars. When he cried, the seven thunders uttered their voices. When the seven thunders sounded, I was about to write; but I heard a voice from the sky saying, "Seal up the things which the seven thunders said, and don't write them." The angel who I saw standing on the sea and on the land lifted up his right hand to the sky, and swore by him who lives forever and ever, who created heaven and the things that are in it, the earth and the things that are in it, and the sea and the things that are in it, that there will no longer be delay, but in the days of the voice of the seventh angel, when he is about to sound, then the mystery of God is finished, as he declared to his servants, the prophets. The voice which I heard from heaven, again speaking with me, said, "Go, and take the book which is open in the hand of the angel who stands on the sea and on the land." I went to the angel, saying, "Give me the little book." He said to me, "Take it, and eat it up. It will make your belly bitter, but in your mouth it will be as sweet as honey." I took the little book out of the angel's hand, and ate it up. It was as sweet as honey in my mouth. When I had eaten it, my belly was made bitter. He told me, "You must prophesy again over many peoples, nations, languages, and kings" (Rev 10 WEB).

The Lord reveals a vision to John and then tells him to seal it up and not write it down. This chapter depicts Christ getting ready to usher in His reign on earth (Rev. 10:1). John saw a mighty angel coming down from heaven, clothed in clouds with a rainbow around His head. His feet were like pillars of fire. I believe this is a description of Jesus. Acts 1:11 tells us that Christ will come again in the clouds. Also, a rainbow is a symbol of God's covenant with Noah, and the description of His face like a pillar of fire fits the description of Christ in Revelation 1:13–16. In Revelation 10:2 He has a little book, or scroll, which represents the title deed to the earth. John is told: "Take it, and eat it up. It will make your belly bitter, but in your mouth it will be as sweet as honey" (Rev. 10:9 WEB).

The instructions mean that John should consume (read) the book. What John reads (the promise to the believer) is sweet, yet the calamities that are to come upon the earth and its non-believing inhabitants are very bitter and discomforting. Next, John is told, "You must prophesy again over many peoples, nations, languages, and kings" (Rev. 10:11 WEB).

These are John's instructions for writing the book of Revelation so that all the world can read the prophecies of this book.

Chapter Eleven

> A reed like a rod was given to me. One said, "Rise, and measure God's temple, and the altar, and those who worship in it. Leave out the court which is outside of the temple, and don't measure it, for it has been given to the gentiles. They will tread the holy city under foot for forty-two months. I will give power to my two witnesses, and they will prophesy one thousand two hundred sixty days, clothed in sackcloth. These are the two olive trees and the two lampstands, standing before the Lord of the earth. If anyone desires to harm them, fire proceeds out of their mouth and devours their enemies. If anyone desires to harm them, he must be killed in this way. These have the power to shut up the sky that it may not rain during the days of their prophecy. They have power over the waters, to turn them into blood, and to strike

the earth with every plague, as often as they desire. When they have finished their testimony, the beast that comes up out of the abyss will make war with them, and overcome them, and kill them. Their dead bodies will be in the street of the great city, which spiritually is called Sodom and Egypt, where also their Lord was crucified. From among the peoples, tribes, languages, and nations will people look at their dead bodies for three and a half days, and will not allow their dead bodies to be laid in a tomb. Those who dwell on the earth will rejoice over them, and make merry. They will send gifts to one another, because these two prophets tormented those who dwell on the earth. After the three and a half days, the breath of life from God entered into them, and they stood on their feet. Great fear fell on those who saw them. I heard a loud voice from heaven saying to them, "Come up here! "They went up into heaven in the cloud, and their enemies saw them. In that hour, there was a great earthquake, and a tenth of the city fell. Seven thousand people were killed in the earthquake, and the rest were terrified, and gave glory to the God of heaven. The second woe is past. Behold, the third woe comes quickly. The seventh angel sounded, and there followed great voices in heaven, saying, "The kingdom of the world has become the kingdom of our Lord, and of his Christ. He will reign forever and ever!" The twenty-four elders, who sit before God on their thrones, fell on their faces and worshiped God, saying: "We give you thanks, Lord God, the Almighty, the one who is and who was; because you have taken your great power, and reigned. The nations were angry, and your wrath came, as did the time for the dead to be judged, and to give your servants, the prophets, their reward, as well as the saints, and those who fear your name, the small and the great; and to destroy those who destroy the earth." God's temple that is in heaven was opened, and the ark of the

Lord's covenant was seen in his temple. There followed lightnings, sounds, thunders, an earthquake, and great hail" (Rev 11 WEB).

At the beginning of this chapter, John is instructed to measure the temple of God but to leave the outer court unmeasured because it will be given to the Gentiles, and they will tread the outer court for forty-two months (three and a half years). There are some very profound facts in these verses. First off, we know from the text that there will be a temple; secondly, we are told the outer court will be given to the Gentiles and they will tread the city for forty-two months. So—what does this mean in modern-day events? In Daniel 9 we are told that the world leader will confirm a treaty between Israel and Palestine so the Jews can rebuild their temple. The temple is to be built next to the Dome of the Rock Mosque, which is presently located in the outer court. We know there is no way that the Muslims' Dome of the Rock Mosque can be removed without a holy war. The book of Ezekiel informs us that there will be a wall separating the two.

Next, we read that the city (Jerusalem) will be treaded on by the Gentiles for forty-two months. (Note: when the Holy Spirit gives exact days and times, take heed to His specific warning.) The Muslims controlled Jerusalem prior to 1967. The Jews needed to take possession of the city before the prophecy could be fulfilled, and it happened in 1967. Israel is a time-clock for God's prophetic plans.

Forty-two months is in reference to the abomination of desolation, which is when the Antichrist will walk into the temple and demand to be worshipped. From then it will be forty-two months (or 1,290 days) until the end.

Verses 3 to 10 tell of the two witnesses sent by God to proclaim their testimony: "I will give power to my two witnesses, and they will prophesy one thousand two hundred sixty days, clothed in sackcloth" (Rev. 11:3). We can assume that, because sackcloth and ashes were the garments of the prophets when they mourned for nations, these witnesses are sent to the Jews to testify about Christ. In Malachi 4:5 the Lord says, "Behold, I will send you Elijah the prophet before the coming of the great and dreadful day of the LORD."

Then later on Christ said John the Baptist was a type of Elijah: "Indeed, Elijah is coming first and will restore all things" (Matt. 17:11 NKJV). He may have been referring to this same verse. Therefore, the Scriptures testify to Elijah being one of the witnesses.

Although the other witness is not named, most scholars believe it will be Enoch (because Enoch and Elijah never died) or Moses. We are told that the two witnesses will be protected by God and cannot be harmed until after their testimony is complete. Then, and only then, can the Antichrist (representing the one from the abyss) have them killed and then proceed to leave their bodies on display for three and a half days. We are also told that the world will celebrate this event as if it were a national or global holiday. Suddenly, to everyone's astonishment, the two witnesses arise and ascend into heaven with the whole world witnessing.

Next will come the seventh trumpet; the angels proclaim, "The second woe is past. Behold, the third woe comes quickly" (Rev. 11:14 WEB).

And loud voices in heaven will resound, saying, "The kingdom of the world has become the kingdom of our Lord, and of his Christ. He will reign forever and ever!" (Rev. 11:15 WEB).

The Temple of God will be opened in heaven. As stated earlier, Revelation is laid out systematically. Some chapters depict what will happen in heaven, while others describe what will happen on Earth. Therefore, the book is not written in complete chronological order. Some chapters may be offering a review of past prophecies and past events. Keeping this in mind, let's move into chapter 12.

Chapter Twelve

A great sign was seen in heaven: a woman clothed with the sun, and the moon under her feet, and on her head a crown of twelve stars. She was with child. She cried out, laboring and in pain, giving birth. Another sign was seen in heaven. Behold, a great red dragon, having seven heads and ten horns, and on his heads seven crowns. His tail drew one third of the stars of the sky, and threw them to the earth. The dragon stood before the woman who was about to give birth, so that when she gave birth he might devour her child. She gave birth to a son, a male child, who is to rule all the nations with a rod of iron. Her child was caught up to God, and to his throne. The woman fled into the wilderness, where she has a place prepared by God, that there they may nourish her one thousand two hundred sixty days. There was war in the sky. Michael and his angels made war on the dragon. The dragon and his angels made war. They didn't prevail, neither was a place found for him any more in heaven. The great dragon was thrown down, the old serpent, he who is called the Devil and Satan, the deceiver of the whole world. He was thrown down to the earth, and his angels were thrown down with him. I heard a loud voice in heaven, saying, "Now is come the salvation, the power, and the kingdom of our God, and the authority of his Christ; for the accuser of our brothers has been thrown down, who accuses them before our God day and night. They overcame him because of the Lamb's blood, and because of the word of their testimony. They didn't love their life, even to death. Therefore rejoice, heavens, and you who dwell in them. Woe for the earth and for the sea, because the devil has gone down to you, having great wrath, knowing that he has but a short time." When the dragon saw that he was thrown down to the earth, he persecuted the woman who gave birth to the male child. Two wings of the great eagle were given to the woman that she might fly into the wilderness to her place, where she was nourished for a time, and times, and half a time from the face of the serpent. The serpent spewed water out of his mouth after the woman like a river that he might cause her to be carried away by the stream. The earth helped the woman, and the earth opened its mouth and swallowed up the river which the dragon spewed out of his mouth. The dragon grew angry with the woman, and went away to make war with the rest of her seed, who keep God's commandments and hold Jesus' testimony (Rev. 12 WEB).

The first verse presents the nation of Israel, whereas verses 2 to 5 present the promise of a "savior" and Satan's plan to wipe out the plan of redemption, as well as the fallen angels being cast out of heaven (as alluded to in chapter 8). Verse 6 speaks of Israel fleeing to the wilderness (Petra) after the abomination of desolation. Verse 7 declares a mighty war in heaven, where Satan and his fallen angels fight with Michael and the Lord's angels, but they will not prevail. Satan and his angels are cast to the earth. (Here in chapter 12 John is giving a recap of the previous prophetic events.) He continues, "Woe to the inhabitants of the earth and the sea! For the devil has come down to you, having great wrath, because he knows that he has a short time" (Rev. 12:12 NKJV).

Can you imagine how horrifying it will be for the people of the earth? The full power of Satan will be unleashed, without the Spirit of God to defend them. God has repeatedly promised His nation Israel that He will provide refuge for His people, and in verses 13 to 17 God again promised His Spirit of protection to His children and that He will lead them into the wilderness. (Note from the book of Daniel: we are told that during the last seven years the Spirit of God will be upon the nation of Israel.)

Chapter Thirteen

Then I stood on the sand of the sea. I saw a beast coming up out of the sea, having ten horns and seven heads. On his horns were ten crowns, and on his heads, blasphemous names. The beast which I saw was like a leopard, and his feet were like those of a bear, and his mouth like the mouth of a lion. The dragon gave him his power, his throne, and great authority. One of his heads looked like it had been wounded fatally. His fatal wound was healed, and the whole earth marveled at the beast. They worshiped the dragon, because he gave his authority to the beast, and they worshiped the beast, saying, "Who is like the beast? Who is able to make war with him?" A mouth speaking great things and blasphemy was given to him. Authority to continue for forty-two months was given to him. He opened his mouth for blasphemy against God, to blaspheme his name, and his tent, those who dwell in heaven. It was given to him to make war with the saints, and to overcome them. Authority over every tribe, people, language, and nation was given to him. All who dwell on the earth will worship him, everyone whose name has not been written from the foundation of the world in the book of life of the Lamb who has been killed. If anyone has an ear, let him hear. If anyone gathers into captivity, into captivity he goes. If anyone will kill with the sword, with the sword he must be killed. Here is the patience and the faith of the saints. I saw another beast coming up out of the earth. He had two horns like a lamb, and he spoke like a dragon. He exercises all the authority of the first beast in his presence. He makes the earth and those who dwell in it to worship the first beast, whose fatal wound was healed. He performs great signs, even making fire come down out of the sky on the earth in the sight of men. He deceives my own people who dwell on the earth because of the signs which it was given him to do in front of the beast; saying to those who dwell on the earth, that they should make an image to the beast who had the sword wound and lived. It was given to him to give breath to it, to the image of the beast, that the image of the beast should both speak, and cause as many as wouldn't worship the image of the beast to be killed. He causes all, the small and the great, the rich and the poor, and the free and the slave, to be given a mark on their right hand, or on their forehead; and that no one would be able to buy or to sell, unless he has that mark, the name of the beast or the number of his name. Here is wisdom. He who has understanding, let him calculate the number of the beast, for it is the number of a man. His number is six hundred sixty-six" (Rev. 13 WEB).

Chapter 13 brings in some very profound statements. In fact, it even foretells of a technology that is in the works and is sure to come to pass in the near future. Let's take a look at this exciting chapter.

The first verse says, "I saw a beast rising up out of the sea" (NKJV). This beast is the world leader who will possess demonic powers and will be able to perform signs and wonders. In verse 3, John says, "And I saw one of his heads as if it had been mortally wounded, and his deadly wound was healed. And all the world marveled and followed the beast" (NKJV). The world will worship this leader; they will declare him as the greatest, stating, "Who is like the beast? Who is able to make war with him?" (Rev. 13:4 NKJV).

This beast (world leader, Antichrist) will be exalted and worshipped by the whole world. In verses 5 to 7 we are told that this world leader will be given power to blaspheme God for forty-two months, and he will make war against the saints and overcome them. In the original Greek language, the word here for saints is hagios, which refers to "a person or persons who are ceremonially and or morally pure." From the context, it is believed that this is referring to Israel. Power over all mankind will be given to the Antichrist.

Verse 8 emphasizes that all who dwell on the earth will worship him—everyone, that is, whose name is not written in the book of life. Verse 9: "If anyone has an ear, let him hear" (NKJV). So again, the Holy Spirit is warning us to heed His prophecy.

Moving forward into verses 11 to 14, another beast comes out of the earth and performs signs and wonders and deceives those who dwell on the earth. This man is a "sidekick" to the Antichrist and is thought to be a religious leader. Verses 16 and 17 describe a technology that has only been available since the mid-1980s: "He causes all, both small and great, rich and poor, free and slave, to receive a mark on their right hand or on their foreheads, and that no one may buy or sell except one who has the mark or the name of the beast, or the number of his name" (NKJV). Think about what you just read. Also, keep in mind that the Geneva Bible went to print in 1590, and it contained this same verse. Imagine reading this passage over four hundred years ago; think how far-fetched this technology would seem. Yet today, we have this very technology already in place.

Next the text speaks of the world leader doing away with all currency and setting up a global monetary system by implanting microchips or laser tattoos in people. Without this system, people would not be able to purchase or sell anything. "If anyone has an ear, let him hear" (Rev. 13:9 NKJV). In December 1999 a company went public on NASDAQ selling shares to a patent that enables them to insert microchips into humans for the purpose of E-commerce and global tracking. (Strangely enough, the shares are being traded under the name Digital Angel). Take note that this same leader will force everyone to take the mark. It will be a mandatory system. At its introduction, it may seem like a convenience, not worrying about carrying cash, checks or credit cards. It may be considered trendy for the upper class yet still not be affordable for all. Finally, when he begins to shows his "true colors," he will force all people to cooperate with his one world order.

Look back at history and be reminded that Christ said when you see these things beginning to happen, you should "look up and lift up your heads, because your redemption draws near" (Luke 21:28 NKJV). The Lord is telling us to discern the times and to be prepared. We are also told that during the end times, knowledge will increase. Could this be one of the final signs of the Lord's return?

Chapter Fourteen

> *I saw, and behold, the Lamb standing on Mount Zion, and with him one hundred forty-four thousand, having his name, and the name of his Father, written on their foreheads. I heard a sound from heaven, like the sound of many waters, and like the sound of a great thunder. The sound which I heard was like that of harpers playing on their harps. They sing something like a new song before the throne, and before the four living creatures and the elders. None could learn the song except the one hundred forty-four thousand, those who had been redeemed out of the earth. These are those who were not defiled with women, for they are virgins. These are those who follow the Lamb wherever he goes. These were redeemed by Jesus from among men, the first fruits to God and to the Lamb. In their mouth was found no lie. They are without fault. I saw another angel flying in mid heaven, having an eternal gospel to*

proclaim to those who dwell on the earth, and to every nation, tribe, language, and people. He said with a loud voice, "Fear God, and give him glory; for the hour of his judgment has come. Worship him who made the heaven, the earth, the sea, and the springs of waters!" Another, a second angel, followed, saying, "Babylon the great has fallen, which has made all the nations to drink of the wine of the wrath of her sexual immorality." Another angel, a third, followed them, saying with a great voice, "If anyone worships the beast and his image, and receives a mark on his forehead, or on his hand, he also will drink of the wine of the wrath of God, which is prepared unmixed in the cup of his anger. He will be tormented with fire and sulfur in the presence of the holy angels, and in the presence of the Lamb. The smoke of their torment goes up forever and ever. They have no rest day and night, those who worship the beast and his image, and whoever receives the mark of his name. Here is the patience of the saints, those who keep the commandments of God, and the faith of Jesus." I heard the voice from heaven saying, "Write, 'Blessed are the dead who die in the Lord from now on.' "Yes," says the Spirit, "that they may rest from their labors; for their works follow with them." I looked, and behold, a white cloud; and on the cloud one sitting like a son of man, having on his head a golden crown, and in his hand a sharp sickle. Another angel came out from the temple, crying with a loud voice to him who sat on the cloud, "Send forth your sickle, and reap; for the hour to reap has come; for the harvest of the earth is ripe!" He who sat on the cloud thrust his sickle on the earth, and the earth was reaped. Another angel came out from the temple which is in heaven. He also had a sharp sickle. Another angel came out from the altar, he who has power over fire, and he called with a great voice to him who had the sharp sickle, saying, "Send forth your sharp sickle, and gather the clusters of the vine of the earth, for her grapes are fully ripe!" The angel thrust his sickle into the earth, and gathered the vintage of the earth, and threw it into the great winepress of the wrath of God. The winepress was trodden outside of the city, and blood came out from the winepress, even to the bridles of the horses, as far as one thousand six hundred stadia (Rev 14 WEB).

(Note: A stadia is about sixteen-hundred feet; therefore the total distance is approximately two-hundred miles.]

The 144,000 are taken from Mount Zion in Israel up into heaven and are presented as the first fruits of Israel before the throne. Our Lord proclaims them spotless in His eyes, and they sing a song that is exclusive to them. It is interesting how the first fruits of the church in chapter 5 (the raptured church) sing a song that is exclusive to themselves; now we see the first fruits of Israel doing likewise. In verse 7, an angel goes out and preaches the gospel to all nations, saying, "Fear God, and give him glory; for the hour of his judgment has come" (WEB).

Another angel follows, saying, "Babylon the great has fallen, which has made all the nations to drink of the wine of the wrath of her sexual immorality" (Rev. 14:8 WEB).

This verse is talking about the Babylonian religious system, which involved worshipping other gods. A third angel follows, saying, "If anyone worships the beast and his image, and receives a mark on his forehead, or on his hand, he also will drink of the wine of the wrath of God" (Rev 14:9–10 WEB).

Yet this angel goes on to say in verses 12 and 13 that those who do not take the mark and who die for the Lord's sake will be blessed and have rest from their labor. This text is referring to anyone in the tribulation who refuses to take the mark; they will be killed for their commitment to Christ.

Revelation 14:14–20 is actually John's vision of the battle of Armageddon (see Isaiah 63). Christ is to come on a white cloud, and the final wrath of the Lamb will be poured out upon the earth. (More on this in later chapters.)

Chapter Fifteen

> *I saw another great and marvelous sign in the sky: seven angels having the seven last plagues, for in them God's wrath is finished. I saw something like a sea of glass mixed with fire, and those who overcame the beast, and his image, and the number of his name, standing on the sea of glass, having harps of God. They sang the song of Moses, the servant of God, and the song of the Lamb, saying, "Great and marvelous are your works, Lord God, the Almighty; Righteous and true are your ways, you King of the nations. Who wouldn't fear you, Lord, And glorify your name? For you only are holy. For all the nations will come and worship before you. For your righteous acts have been revealed. After these things I looked, and the temple of the tent of the testimony in heaven was opened. The seven angels who had the seven plagues came out from the temple, clothed with pure, bright linen, and wearing golden sashes around their breasts. One of the four living creatures gave to the seven angels seven golden bowls full of the wrath of God, who lives forever and ever. The temple was filled with smoke from the glory of God, and from his power. No one was able to enter into the temple, until the seven plagues of the seven angels would be finished (Rev 15 WEB).*

Chapter 15 is a review chapter. In it, John gets another glimpse of the heavenly scene, and he sees the seven angels ready to pour out the last seven plagues. The final torment will be the last three and half years of the world's existence; then Christ will return with His church. Notice that in verses 2 to 4 there is a multitude of people in heaven who had victory over the beast, over his image and over his mark.

Continuing on, the victorious group is heard singing the song of Moses the bond-servant, the same song given to the Israelites when they crossed the Red Sea in Exodus 15:1–21. In verses 5 to 8 we notice the temple of the tabernacle in heaven being opened and the seven angels, along with the four living creatures, preparing the golden bowls of the wrath of God. God's power and glory are so overwhelming, the temple seems to be filled with smoke.

While chapter 15 of Revelation is a heavenly scene, chapter 16 deals with the events that will take place on earth.

Chapter Sixteen

I heard a loud voice out of the temple, saying to the seven angels, "Go and pour out the seven bowls of the wrath of God on the earth!" The first went, and poured out his bowl into the earth, and it became a harmful and evil sore on the men who had the mark of the beast, and who worshiped his image. The second angel poured out his bowl into the sea, and it became blood as of a dead man. Every living thing in the sea died. The third poured out his bowl into the rivers and springs of water, and it became blood. I heard the angel of the waters saying, "You are righteous, who are and who were, you Holy One, because you judged this way. For they poured out the blood of the saints and the prophets, and you have given them blood to drink. They deserve this." I heard the altar saying, "Yes, Lord God, the Almighty, true and righteous are your judgments." The fourth poured out his bowl on the sun, and it was given to him to scorch men with fire. Men were scorched with great heat, and they blasphemed the name of God who has the power over these plagues. They didn't repent and give him glory. The fifth poured out his bowl on the throne of the beast, and his kingdom was darkened. They gnawed their tongues because of the pain, and they blasphemed the God of heaven because of their pains and their sores. They didn't repent of their works. The sixth poured out his bowl on the great river, the Euphrates. Its water was dried up, that the way might be made ready for the kings that come from the sunrise. I saw coming out of the mouth of the dragon, and out of the mouth of the beast, and out of the mouth of the false prophet, three unclean spirits, something like frogs; for they are spirits of demons, performing signs; which go forth to the kings of the whole world, to gather them together for the war of the great day of God, the Almighty. "Behold, I come like a thief. Blessed is he who watches, and keeps his clothes, so that he doesn't walk naked, and they see his shame." He gathered them together into the place which is called in Hebrew, "Harmagedon." The seventh poured out his bowl into the air. A loud voice came forth out of the temple, from the throne, saying, "It is done!" There were lightnings, sounds, and thunders; and there was a great earthquake, such as was not since there were men on the earth, so great an earthquake, so mighty. The great city was divided into three parts, and the cities of the nations fell. Babylon the great was remembered in the sight of God, to give to her the cup of the wine of the fierceness of his wrath. Every island fled away, and the mountains were not found. Great hailstones, about the weight of a talent, came down out of the sky on men. Men blasphemed God because of the plague of the hail, for the plague of it is exceeding great (Rev 16 WEB).

Chapter 16 reveals the last seven plagues, which are the final judgments. Looking at these plagues we can see how today military weapons could causes destruction such as the following:

1. Loathsome and malignant sores upon man, possibly due to a nuclear fallout (verse 2)
2. Contamination of the seas and rivers due to massive deaths caused by chemical warfare (verses 3 and 4)
3. Blocking of the sun and depletion of the ozone layer due to nuclear weapons and fallout, causing intense scorching to humans (verses 8 and 9)

In verse 15 Christ again gives us a warning and a chance to repent: "Behold, I come like a thief. Blessed is he who watches, and keeps his clothes, so that he doesn't walk naked, and they see his shame" (WEB).

In ancient days, the temple guards had to always be awake; if they were caught sleeping, they were beaten and their garments were set on fire. Christ let them know that they do not have to face this tribulation. Instead they can have salvation through Him.

Our job as Christians is to be Christ like and to preach the gospel with love to all the ends of the earth. This is the Great Commission. We need to preach the Gospel and the prophecy of this book so that people will have knowledge and a forewarning of the plagues that are promised to the non-believers.

Chapter Seventeen

One of the seven angels who had the seven bowls came and spoke with me, saying, "Come here. I will show you the judgment of the great prostitute who sits on many waters, with whom the kings of the earth committed sexual immorality, and those who dwell in the earth were made drunken with the wine of her sexual immorality." He carried me away in the Spirit into a wilderness. I saw a woman sitting on a scarlet-colored animal, full of blasphemous names, having seven heads and ten horns. The woman was dressed in purple and scarlet, and decked with gold and precious stones and pearls, having in her hand a golden cup full of abominations, even the unclean things of her sexual immorality, and on her forehead a name written, "MYSTERY, BABYLON THE GREAT, THE MOTHER OF THE PROSTITUTES AND OF THE ABOMINATIONS OF THE EARTH." I saw the woman drunken with the blood of the saints, and with the blood of the martyrs of Jesus. When I saw her, I wondered with great amazement. The angel said to me, "Why do you wonder? I will tell you the mystery of the woman, and of the beast that carries her, which has the seven heads and the ten horns. The beast that you saw was, and is not; and is about to come up out of the abyss, and to go into destruction. Those who dwell on the earth will wonder, whose name has not been written in the book of life from the foundation of the world, when they see the beast, how that he was, and is not, and will come. Here is the mind that has wisdom. The seven heads are seven mountains, on which the woman sits. They are seven kings. Five have fallen, the one is, and the other is not yet come. When he comes, he must continue a little while. The beast that was, and is not, is himself also an eighth, and is of the seven; and he goes to destruction. The ten horns that you saw are ten kings, who have received no kingdom as yet, but they receive authority as kings, with the beast, for one hour. These have one mind, and they give their power and authority to the beast. These will war against the Lamb, and the Lamb will overcome them, for he is Lord of lords, and King of kings. They also will overcome who are with him, called and chosen and faithful." He said to me, "The waters which you saw, where the prostitute sits, are peoples, multitudes, nations, and languages. The ten horns which you saw, and the beast, these will hate the prostitute, and will make her desolate and naked, and will eat her flesh, and will burn her utterly with fire. For

God has put in their hearts to do what he has in mind, and to come to unity of mind, and to give their kingdom to the beast, until the words of God should be accomplished. The woman whom you saw is the great city, which reigns over the kings of the earth" (Rev. 17 WEB).

We read of the scarlet woman and the beast. This chapter is referring to a religious system, which has been referred to earlier as "Babylon." (Read Hislop's The Two Babylons for more information. As stated earlier, religion is man's way to reach God, whereas the Bible—or God's Word—is God's way to reach man.) In the early years of Christianity, the government decided to establish a religion, which was soon corrupted by Babylonian traditions. In verses 2 to 9, the Roman Empire, headed by the Antichrist, will join forces with this religious leader—the False Prophet. The Antichrist and False Prophet will form a false global religion, and they will deceive the world.

In verses 10 and 11, a demonic spirit will come out of the abyss and enter into this world leader. He is a possessed by one of the seven Roman emperors. (Some scholars believe it to be the same demonic spirit that possessed Nero Claudius Caesar, who was known by the early church as "the beast.") In verses 12 and 13, ten kings join together and give power to "the Beast." This alliance is already in process today; the countries of Europe have joined together as one. From out of them will rise the world leader known here in Scriptures as "the beast." Continuing in verses 14 to 18, this great kingdom and religious system under "the beast" will make war with the Lamb of God—yet he will not prevail.

In chapter 17 we see the destruction of the religious system or the spiritual Babylon; in chapter 18 we have the physical destruction of the city of Babylon.

Chapter Eighteen

After these things, I saw another angel coming down out of the sky, having great authority. The earth was illuminated with his glory. He cried with a mighty voice, saying, "Fallen, fallen is Babylon the great, and has become a habitation of demons, and a prison of every unclean spirit, and a prison of every unclean and hateful bird! For all the nations have drunk of the wine of the wrath of her sexual immorality, the kings of the earth committed sexual immorality with her, and the merchants of the earth grew rich from the abundance of her luxury." I heard another voice from heaven, saying, "Come forth, my people, out of her, that you have no participation in her sins, and that you don't receive of her plagues, for her sins have reached to the sky, and God has remembered her iniquities. Return to her just as she returned, and double to her the double according to her works. In the cup which she mixed, mix to her double. However much she glorified herself, and grew wanton, so much give her of torment and mourning. For she says in her heart, 'I sit a queen, and am no widow, and will in no way see mourning.' Therefore in one day her plagues will come: death, mourning, and famine; and she will be utterly burned with fire; for the Lord God who has judged her is strong. The kings of the earth, who committed sexual immorality and lived wantonly with her, will weep and wail over her, when they look at the smoke of her burning, standing far away for the fear of her torment, saying, 'Woe, woe, the great city, Babylon, the strong city! For your judgment has come in one hour.' The merchants of the earth weep and mourn over her, for no one buys their merchandise anymore; merchandise of gold, silver, precious stones, pearls, fine linen, purple, silk, scarlet, all expensive wood, every vessel of ivory, every vessel made of most precious wood,

204

and of brass, and iron, and marble; and cinnamon, spices, incense, ointment, frankincense, wine, oil, fine flour, wheat, cattle, and sheep; and merchandise of horses and chariots and slaves; and souls of men. The fruits which your soul lusted after have been lost to you, and all things that were dainty and sumptuous have perished from you, and you will find them no more at all. The merchants of these things, who were made rich by her, will stand far away for the fear of her torment, weeping and mourning; saying, 'Woe, woe, the great city, she who was dressed in fine linen, purple, and scarlet, and decked with gold and precious stones and pearls! For in an hour such great riches are made desolate.' Every shipmaster, and everyone who sails anywhere, and mariners, and as many as gain their living by sea, stood far away, and cried out as they looked at the smoke of her burning, saying, 'What is like the great city?' They cast dust on their heads, and cried, weeping and mourning, saying, 'Woe, woe, the great city, in which all who had their ships in the sea were made rich by reason of her great wealth!' For in one hour is she made desolate. Rejoice over her, O heaven, you saints, you apostles, and you prophets; for God has judged your judgment on her." A mighty angel took up a stone like a great millstone and cast it into the sea, saying, "Thus with violence will Babylon, the great city, be thrown down, and will be found no more at all. The voice of harpers and minstrels and flute players and trumpeters will be heard no more at all in you. No craftsman, of whatever craft, will be found any more at all in you. The sound of a mill will be heard no more at all in you. The light of a lamp will shine no more at all in you. The voice of the bridegroom and of the bride will be heard no more at all in you; for your merchants were the princes of the earth; for with your sorcery all the nations were deceived. In her was found the blood of prophets and of saints, and of all who have been slain on the earth" (Rev. 18 WEB).

It is worthy to note that today's Iraq was formerly Babylon. In fact, Saddam Hussein was in the process of restoring Baghdad into the image of Nebuchadnezzar's dynasty. In verses 9 and 10, the kings of the earth grieve over Babylon's destruction and stand far off for fear of its torment as they see the smoke rise.

Verses 17 to 19 tell that in one hour the city will be totally decimated. This is a good description of a nuclear-style war— cities being destroyed in one hour, kings watching from a distance and feeling tormented. Could it be that the torment and watching at a distance depicts nuclear fallout? Again, you must keep in mind that when John wrote this book, bows and arrows, swords and stones were the weapons of warfare.

In verse 20 those in heaven are told to rejoice over Babylon, for God hath avenged her. It is also interesting that the Bible is a tale of two cities: Jerusalem and Babylon. The final torment is over, as expressed in verses 21 to 24.

Chapter Nineteen

After these things I heard something like a loud voice of a great multitude in heaven, saying, "Hallelujah! Salvation, glory, and power belong to our God: for true and righteous are his judgments. For he has judged the great prostitute, her who corrupted the earth with her sexual immorality, and he has avenged the blood of his servants at her hand." A second time they said, "Hallelujah! Her smoke goes up forever and ever." The twenty-four elders and the four living creatures fell down and worshiped God who sits on the throne, saying, "Amen! Hallelujah!" A voice came forth from the throne, saying, "Give praise to our God, all you his servants, you who fear him, the small and the great!" I heard something like the voice of a great multitude, and like the voice of many waters, and like the voice of mighty thunders, saying, "Hallelujah! For the Lord our God, the Almighty, reigns! Let us rejoice and be exceedingly glad, and let us give the glory to him. For the marriage of the Lamb has come, and his wife has made herself ready." It was given to her that she would array herself in bright, pure, fine linen: for the fine linen is the righteous acts of the saints. He said to me, "Write, 'Blessed are those who are invited to the marriage supper of the Lamb.'" He said to me, "These are true words of God." I fell down before his feet to worship him. He said to me, "Look! Don't do it! I am a fellow bondservant with you and with your brothers who hold the testimony of Jesus. Worship God, for the testimony of Jesus is the Spirit of Prophecy." I saw the heaven opened, and behold, a white horse, and he who sat on it is called Faithful and True. In righteousness he judges and makes war. His eyes are a flame of fire, and on his head are many crowns. He has names written and a name written which no one knows but he himself. He is clothed in a garment sprinkled with blood. His name is called "The Word of God." The armies which are in heaven followed him on white horses, clothed in white, pure, fine linen. Out of his mouth proceeds a sharp, two-edged sword, that with it he should strike the nations. He will rule them with a rod of iron. He treads the winepress of the fierceness of the wrath of God, the Almighty. He has on his garment and on his thigh a name written, "KING OF KINGS, AND LORD OF LORDS." I saw an angel standing in the sun. He cried with a loud voice, saying to all the birds that fly in the sky, "Come! Be gathered together to the great supper of God, that you may eat the flesh of kings, the flesh of captains, the flesh of mighty men, and the flesh of horses and of those who sit on them, and the flesh of all men, both free and slave, and small and great." I saw the beast, and the kings of the earth, and their armies, gathered together to make war against him who sat on the horse, and against his army. The beast was taken, and with him the false prophet who worked the signs in his sight, with which he deceived those who had received the mark of the beast and those who worshiped his image. They two were thrown alive into the lake of fire that burns with sulfur. The rest were killed with the sword of him who sat on the horse, the sword which came forth out of his mouth. All the birds were filled with their flesh" (Rev 19 WEB).

After two chapters about the religious and the physical destruction of Babylon, chapter 19 begins by describing the praise and worship that will take place in heaven. In verses 5 to 10, those in heaven are gathered together for the Marriage Supper of the Lamb and blessed.

In verses 11 through 16, the heavens open and the great rider of the white horse (Jesus Christ) appears. He is called Faithful and True. He is clothed in a white vesture that was dipped in blood, and out of His mouth came the Word of God (like a sharp sword). He is the King over all kings and the Lord over all lords. Now is the time to return to the earth with His army (the Church). This is known as The Second Coming of Christ.

Next, we have the culmination of the Battle of Armageddon, where the Antichrist, the False Prophet and Satan gather together with the kings of the earth for the final battle in the Valley of Megiddo. It is at this point that Jesus will speak the Word of God and destroy them all.

The Divine Outline

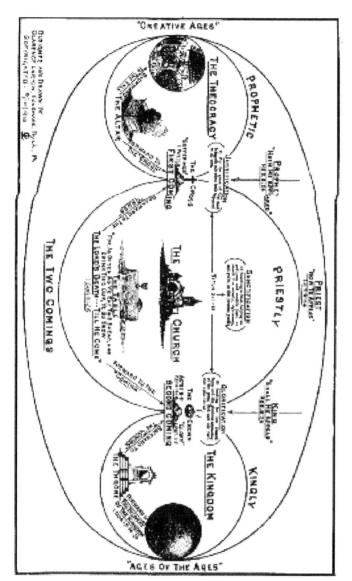

209

Chapter Twenty

I saw an angel coming down out of heaven, having the key of the abyss and a great chain in his hand. He seized the dragon, the old serpent, which is the Devil and Satan, and bound him for one thousand years, and cast him into the abyss, and shut it, and sealed it over him, that he should deceive the nations no more, until the thousand years were finished. After this, he must be freed for a short time. I saw thrones, and they sat on them, and judgment was given to them. I saw the souls of those who had been beheaded for the testimony of Jesus, and for the word of God, and such as didn't worship the beast nor his image, and didn't receive the mark on their forehead and on their hand. They lived, and reigned with Christ one thousand years. The rest of the dead didn't live until the thousand years were finished. This is the first resurrection. Blessed and holy is he who has part in the first resurrection. Over these, the second death has no power, but they will be priests of God and of Christ, and will reign with him one thousand years. And after the thousand years, Satan will be freed out of his prison, and will come forth to deceive the nations which are in the four corners of the earth, Gog and Magog, to gather them together to the war; the number of whom is as the sand of the sea. They went up over the breadth of the earth, and surrounded the camp of the saints, and the beloved city. Fire came down out of heaven, and devoured them. The devil who deceived them was thrown into the lake of fire and sulfur, where are also the beast and the false prophet. They will be tormented day and night forever and ever. I saw a great white throne, and him who sat on it, from whose face the earth and the heaven fled away. There was found no place for them. I saw the dead, the great and the small, standing before the throne. Books were opened. Another

*book was opened, which is the book of life. The dead
were judged out of the things which were written in the
books, according to their works. The sea gave up the
dead who were in it. Death and Hades gave up the dead
who were in them. They were judged, each one
according to his works. Death and Hades were thrown
into the lake of fire. This is the second death, the lake of
fire. If anyone was not found written in the book of life,
he was cast into the lake of fire (Rev 20 WEB).*

In the first verses of this chapter, Satan is bound in the
bottomless pit for 1,000 years. Yet, after 1,000 years he must
be released. I was always puzzled by this passage. I asked
myself, Why would Satan be held and then let loose? The
answer is simple: God did not create robots; He created us
with free will. During the 1,000 years that Satan is bound,
Christ will reign on earth. During His reign there will be no
temptation. After Satan is released he will have one last chance
to tempt the people who do not have true hearts for the Lord.

Verses 4 to 6 describes what is called the "1,000-year reign
of Christ." Christ will reign on earth with His church (the
raptured saints) as well as the believers who were martyred
for their faith. We also know from the text that there will be
some who survive the great tribulation and live in the
1,000year reign. During these 1,000 years, families will
multiply, and there will be people raised in this perfect
environment who do not know of sin.

Verses 7 to 10 say Satan will be released one more time,
and he will go and prepare an army against God. Then God will
send down fire from heaven and destroy Satan and his
followers. Satan and the False Prophet will be cast into the lake
of fire and brimstone, there to be tormented day and night
forever.

Verses 11 to 15 tell of the Great White Throne of Judgment. All who have died will receive their final judgment, and anyone not found in the book of life will be cast into the lake of fire along with Satan, the False Prophet and all his demons.

Chapter 21 describes the moment that all Christians have been waiting for.

Chapter Twenty-One

I saw a new heaven and a new earth: for the first heaven and the first earth have passed away, and the sea is no more. I saw the holy city, New Jerusalem, coming down out of heaven from God, made ready as a bride adorned for her husband. I heard a loud voice out of heaven saying, "Behold, God's tent is with men, and he will dwell with them, and they will be his people, and God himself will be with them as their God. He will wipe away every tear from their eyes. Death will be no more; neither will there be mourning, nor crying, nor pain, any more. The first things have passed away. He who sits on the throne said, "Behold, I make all things new." He said, "Write, for these words are faithful and true." He said to me, "It is done! I am the Alpha and the Omega, the Beginning and the End. I will give freely to him who is thirsty from the spring of the water of life. He who overcomes, I will give him these things. I will be his God, and he will be my son. But for the cowardly, unbelieving, sinners, abominable, murderers, sexually immoral, sorcerers, idolaters, and all liars, their part is in the lake that burns with fire and sulfur, which is the second death." One of the seven angels who had the seven bowls, who were laden with the seven last plagues came, and he spoke with me, saying, "Come here. I will show you the wife, the Lamb's bride." He carried me away in the Spirit to a great and high mountain, and shown me the holy city, Jerusalem, coming down out of heaven from

God, having the glory of God. Her light was like a most precious stone, as if it was a jasper stone, clear as crystal; having a great and high wall; having twelve gates, and at the gates twelve angels; and names written on them, which are the names of the twelve tribes of the children of Israel. On the east were three gates; and on the north three gates; and on the south three gates; and on the west three gates. The wall of the city had twelve foundations, and on them twelve names of the twelve Apostles of the Lamb. He who spoke with me had for a measure a golden reed to measure the city, its gates, and its walls. The city lies foursquare, and its length is as great as its breadth. He measured the city with the reed, twelve thousand stadia. Its length, breadth, and height are equal. He measured its wall, one hundred forty-four cubits, by the measure of a man, that is, of an angel. The construction of its wall was jasper. The city was pure gold, like pure glass. The foundations of the city's wall were adorned with all kinds of precious stones. The first foundation was jasper; the second, sapphire; the third, chalcedony; the fourth, emerald; the fifth, sardonyx; the sixth, sardius; the seventh, chrysolite; the eighth, beryl; the ninth, topaz; the tenth, chrysoprasus; the eleventh, jacinth; and the twelfth, amethyst. The twelve gates were twelve pearls. Each one of the gates was made of one pearl. The street of the city was pure gold, like transparent glass. I saw no temple in it, for the Lord God, the Almighty, and the Lamb, are its temple. The city has no need for the sun, neither of the moon, to shine, for the very glory of God illuminated it, and its lamp is the Lamb. The nations will walk in its light. The kings of the earth bring their glory into it. Its gates will in no way be shut by day (for there will be no night there), and they will bring the glory and the honor of the nations into it. There will in no way enter into it anything profane, or one who causes an abomination or a lie, but only those who are written in the Lamb's book of life (Rev. 21 WEB).

Here is described the glorious New Jerusalem with the presence of God. Our God will dwell with us forever, His love will be fully manifested in His people, and His glory will be put upon us. There will be no more death, no more pain or suffering; and, all our tears shall be wiped away. The promises of our Lord will have now been fulfilled.

In chapter 22 we have a more detailed description of this heavenly city, as well as a vision of the tree of life in the middle of the street.

Chapter Twenty-Two

He showed me a river of water of life, clear as crystal, proceeding out of the throne of God and of the Lamb, in the midst of its street. On this side of the river and on that was the tree of life, bearing twelve kinds of fruits, yielding its fruit every month. The leaves of the tree were for the healing of the nations. There will be no curse any more. The throne of God and of the Lamb will be in it, and his servants will serve him. They will see his face, and his name will be on their foreheads. There will be no more night, and they need no lamp light, neither sunlight; for the Lord God will give them light. They will reign forever and ever. He said to me, "These words are faithful and true. The Lord, the God of the spirits of the prophets, sent his angels to show to his servants the things which must happen soon." "Behold, I come quickly. Blessed is he who keeps the words of the prophecy of this book." Now I, John, am the one who heard and saw these things. When I heard and saw, I fell down to worship before the feet of the angel who had shown me these things. He said to me, "See you don't do it! I am a fellow bondservant with you and with your brothers, the prophets, and with those who keep the words of this book. Worship God." He said to me, "Don't seal up the words of the prophecy of this book, for the time is at hand. He who acts unjustly, let him act unjustly still. He who is filthy, let him be filthy still. He who is righteous, let him do righteousness still. He who is holy, let him be holy still." "Behold, I come quickly. My reward is with me, to repay to each man according to his work. I am the Alpha and the Omega, the First and the Last, the Beginning and the End. Blessed are those who do his commandments that they may have the right to the tree of life, and may enter in by the gates into the city. Outside are the dogs, the sorcerers, the sexually immoral, the murderers, the idolaters, and everyone who loves and practices falsehood. I, Jesus, have sent my angel to testify these things to you for the assemblies. I am the root and the offspring of David; the Bright and Morning Star." The Spirit and the bride say, "Come!" He who hears, let him say, "Come!" He who is thirsty, let him come. He who desires, let him take the water of life freely. I testify to every man who hears the words of the prophecy of this book, if anyone adds to them, may God add to him the plagues which are written in this book. If anyone takes away from the words of the book of this prophecy, may God take away his part from the tree of life, and out of the holy city, which are written in this book. He who testifies these things says, "Yes, I come quickly." Amen! Come, Lord Jesus. The grace of the Lord Jesus be with all the saints. Amen (Rev 22 WEB).

Here all will see Jesus and the Father upon the throne and will be told that all curses are no more. This wonderful city will never have darkness; nor will it need light, for the Lord God gives light forever.

In verses 6 through 20 we have the angel telling John not to seal up this book but to proclaim its message to all. We also have Jesus' confirmation of His Second Coming as He says three times: "Behold, I come quickly."

Blessed are those who obey His commandments, that they might have the right to the tree of life. This is the conclusion of the Bible.

Come quickly, Lord Jesus!

My prayer is that the Holy Spirit through these studies has revealed fresh insights into this majestically prophetic book. But, until the Lord's return, there will still be confusion about all the allegories and word pictures in this text.

In bringing this study to a close, the final section will show parallels with other books of the Bible in order to clarify some of the meaning of the text. Again, remember that the Author (the Holy Spirit) desires that we receive and understand the entire Bible and that we be prepared for the finale. So let's get started. The book of Revelation is about redemption, which means "restoring what was lost to its original owner." The Bible begins with Genesis and ends with Revelation. Genesis represents the beginning with God, whereas Revelation represents completion with God. Taking a closer look at this, we have Genesis 1:1 where "God created the heaven and the earth," while in Revelation 21:1 the earth passes away. In Genesis 1:5 darkness is established, and in Revelation 22:5 darkness is no more. Sin is introduced in Genesis 3; in Revelation 21 and 22, sin is no more. In Genesis 10:8–10, Nimrod founded Babylon, and in Revelation 17 and 18 we have the destruction of Babylon. In Genesis 3:24, man's dominion ceases and Satan's dominion of the earth begins. In Revelation 22, Satan's dominion is ended and man's is restored. These are just a few examples of the parallels between these two dynamic books within the Holy Bible. Let's take a look at the description of our Lord and Savior, Jesus Christ, as found throughout both the Old and New Testaments. In Revelation

1:13–16 we read of Christ as the high priest. He is described in the following ways:

- ❖ He is the intercessor for our sins (Heb. 7:25).

- ❖ He is the one who cleanses us (1 John 1:9).

- ❖ He is our advocate (1 John 2:1).

- ❖ He is the inspector of our fruit (Rev. 2 and 3).

- ❖ He appears in the midst of the seven lamp stands. (The word for lampstand is Luchina, which means "light bearer" or "people who bear His light." See Matthew 5:14–16.)

- ❖ He is clothed with a garment (see Psalm 104:1–2 and Isaiah 11:5).

His chest is girded with a golden band. His head and hair are as white as wool, and His eyes are like a flame of fire. This is parallel to Matthew 17:2 and Daniel 7:9. In His right hand He has seven stars. We are told in Revelation 1:20 that the seven stars are angels. The word for angels here is angelos, which means "messengers" or "believers." (See John 10:28–29.) Out of his mouth comes a sharp two-edged sword—the Word of God (Eph. 6:17; Isa.11:4; Isa. 49:2; Rev. 2–16). His countenance is as the sun. Christ is the light of the world!

In the next chapters, John writes about the seven churches, and in many instances they parallel the churches in the Pauline letters.

First, the church of Ephesus shares a lot of similarities with the church in the book of Ephesians. Ephesians was written to the early church to confront them about heresy and problems in the church. In Ephesians 6:10–17 we are told about the armor of God and how to defend ourselves. The basic setting of the book is to strengthen the believers in their Christian faith. The instructions to the church of Ephesus in Revelation and to the church of Ephesus in Ephesians both deal with the basic nature of the church and the challenges facing the living body of Christ on earth. They need to avoid getting caught up in the world.

Secondly, let's parallel Smyrna with the Philippians. Smyrna was the faithful church whose believers were persecuted unto death, whereas Philippians is a book that boasts about the church having joy in all things. Paul wrote this book while he was in jail, and he emphasized the joy of the Lord. He said that Christ suffered and died for them and that they must stand firm and run the race of Christianity for Him. They must be filled with the fruits of righteousness and have boldness to speak the Word of God without fear.

Pergamos is third and can be related to the Corinthians. In Paul's letters to the Corinthians, one of his main issues was that the Corinthians were married to the world. They lived their lives accepting worldly values and lifestyles and were also caught in false teachings with compromised faith.

Fourth is the church of Thyatira, which shares the same theme as the book of Galatians: the struggle between the gospel and religion. The book of Galatians was written to bring the believers back to the whole gospel. Salvation is received through God's grace, not by legalism or religion. God's children are free in Christ and are guided by His Holy Spirit. The Holy Spirit instructs, leads and gives power. He ends the bondage of religions and creates joy, peace and love that come only through Jesus Christ. The Jews continue to base their faith on the old laws and customs.

Fifth is the church at Sardis. The book of Romans and the passage about Sardis tend to have the same theme, which is that the just must live by faith. Paul gives clear and very descriptive guidelines to the Christian faith. He emphasizes that it is not about theology or law but rather about complete submission to Christ. Paul stressed that salvation and unity come only by the grace that is freely given by our Lord and Savior, Jesus Christ.

Philadelphia (the sixth church) and the book of Thessalonians are parallel as the Raptured church. The church of Philadelphia has the promise of being kept from the hour of tribulation, whereas the book of Thessalonians teaches that Christ is the victor over death. The Thessalonians also accepted the message of the gospel and tested everything that was taught. Paul warned them that Christ could come at any moment and they must be prepared for His coming.

Laodicea (the last church) and the book of Colossians share the same themes. Colossians teaches that Christ needs to be the Lord of life and believers need His guidance every day. The church of Laodicea had Christ standing outside the church, trying to get in. Paul taught that Christ is all things, while the church of Laodicea was caught up in functions and did not have the love of Christ. Paul continually mentions the mystery of Christ, which tells us that the church did not know Him, though they believed they did. It is also interesting to note that the church of Laodicea is mentioned twice in the book of Colossians.

Chapter 4 is referred to as the Rapture chapter. As previously mentioned, this chapter starts with the word "metatuta," which literally means "after these things." John was "caught up." This is parallel to 1 Thessalonians 4:17, which says: "Then we who are alive and remain shall be caught up [harpazios] together with them in the clouds to meet the Lord in the air" (NKJV). This can also be connected with Acts 1:11, which says, "Men of Galilee, why do you stand gazing up into heaven? This same Jesus, who was taken up from you into heaven, will so come in like manner as you saw Him go into heaven" (NKJV).

Now keep in mind that Christ stated in John 11:25, "I am the resurrection and the life. He who believes in Me, though he may die, he shall live" (NKJV). So as you can see, Christ testifies to a generation that will not die. Take note that before John was caught up he heard a voice like a trumpet telling him to come hither. This statement parallels with another Rapture verse found in 1 Corinthians 15:51–52:

> "Behold, I tell you a mystery: We shall not all sleep, but we shall all be changed—in a moment, in the twinkling of an eye, at the last trumpet. For the trumpet will sound, and the dead will be raised incorruptible, and we shall be changed" (NKJV).

Verse 7 speaks of four living creatures: one like a lion, one like a calf (or ox), one with a face like a man and the fourth like an eagle. If we compare the four gospels we will also see some similarities. In Matthew, Christ is presented as the Messiah through the genealogy of Abraham in which Judah was begotten. Judah represents the Lion. Mark presents Jesus as a servant, and in Scriptures a servant is represented by an ox. Luke, being a doctor, presents Jesus' lineage from the root of man (Adam), therefore presenting Jesus as the Son of Man. Finally, John presents Jesus as the Son of God (eagle).

Chapter 5 is known as the Redemption chapter, where Christ is called to open the scroll, which is the title deed to the earth. Christ is the kinsmen redeemer of Adam and has stepped forward to claim what was lost in the Garden of Eden. This chapter has the same theme as the book of Ruth where Boaz (a Jew) marries Ruth (a Gentile) and redeems the land through the genealogy of Naomi's husband. Leviticus 25:23–28 and Jeremiah 32:6–27 both explain the law of property redemption.

In chapter 6, the Church (the body of Christ, believers) is removed from the earth, and a rider on a white horse is introduced. Reflect back to 2 Thessalonians 2:3–12, which talks about the lawless one being at work and waiting to come to power. Yet the restraining force (the body of Christ, believers) is holding him back. Once the Christians are removed, he will be able to come to power. Reading on, note that the rider of the white horse has a bow. The word used here in the Greek is "toxon," which is the same word used in Genesis 9:13. When God gave Noah the promise (covenant) with the rainbow, God used the Hebrew word "keh'sheth" for bow, which stands for a covenant. This is parallel with Daniel 9:27: "Then he shall confirm a covenant with many" (NKJV).

In chapter 6, the world leader is introduced and is followed by wars (Matt. 24:6), famines, pestilence and earthquakes (Matt. 24:7). Verse 9 describes the martyred saints who heard the Word yet were only hearers—not truly Christians. They miss the Rapture and come to faith during the tribulation period. (Keep in mind that the Christians who accept adoption into God's family witness to this group and plant gospel seeds in them prior to the Rapture; see Matthew 24:9–14.) As you can see, Revelation 6 and Matthew 24 share the same content. Skipping over to Revelation 10, here is another description of Jesus Christ. "I saw another mighty angel coming down out of the sky, clothed with a cloud. A rainbow was on his head. His face was like the sun, and his feet like pillars of fire" (Rev. 10:1 WEB).

Now look back at Exodus 24:17 where the glory of the Lord was like a consuming fire. Matthew 24:30 says, "And they will see the Son of Man coming on the clouds" (NKJV).

Chapter 11 starts with John being instructed in the measurements of the temple. This implies that a temple is to be rebuilt. We can cross-reference this with Daniel 9 and Matthew 24:15. (Note: the abomination of desolation refers to making an unclean sacrifice or to the blaspheming of God in His temple or upon the altar of the temple.) In verse 2, John is told not to measure the outer court of the temple because it is given over to the Gentiles. This is a fascinating statement because we know the Dome of the Rock Mosque sits upon the Temple Mount. Prophecies in Ezekiel say there will be a wall put between the Dome and the Temple. Possibly this will institute the world leaders' treaty for peace between the Jews and the Muslims. The world leader will affirm a treaty to rebuild the temple and will divide the temple and the Dome with a wall. This will be his political answer to promoting peace in the Middle East.

Next comes two witnesses who are sent to prophesy, and they are given power from God. Malachi 4:5 says that Elijah will be one of these witnesses. According to Hebrews 9:27, it is appointed once for a man to die. Therefore, scholars believe the other witness could be Enoch because Enoch and Elijah were the only two people in the Bible who never died. "Enoch walked with God; and he was not, for God took him" (Gen. 5:24 NKJV), and Elijah was taken up in a fiery chariot: "Behold, there appeared a chariot of fire and horses of fire which separated the two of them. And Elijah went up by a whirlwind to heaven" (2 Kings 2:11 NASB).

In Revelation 12:4, we have the fall of Satan where he is cast out of heaven. Luke 10:18 and Isaiah 14:12–19 give descriptions of the fall of Satan. In the next verse, a woman representing Israel bears a son (Christ). Then Israel (the woman) flees to the wilderness for 1,260 days. This parallels Daniel 9 in reference to the last three and a half years of the world's history, better known as the "Wrath of the Lamb" or "The Great Tribulation." During this period, full demonic powers will be poured out upon the earth. There will be a war in heaven where Michael and his angels fight against Satan, but Satan will not prevail! (Matt. 16:18).

In chapter 13, a verbal portrait is painted of the beast and his prophet. Another description of the beast can be found in

Daniel 7:3–8. In this scenario there will be an assassination attempt on the world leader's life. Zechariah 11:17 says, "Woe to the worthless shepherd, Who leaves the flock! A sword shall be against his arm, And against his right eye; His arm shall completely wither, And his right eye shall be totally blinded" (NKJV). He makes a miraculous recovery, and the world worships him, saying, "Who is like the beast? Who is able to make war with him?" (Rev. 13:4 WEB).

Chapter 14 starts with Jesus Christ standing on Mount Zion. This parallels Psalm 2:6, "Yet, I have set My King On My holy hill of Zion" (NKJV).

Revelation 14:14 shows the appearing of the Son of Man; He comes for His harvest. This can also be found in the book of Joel when God is judging the nation. Joel 3:13 says, "Put in the sickle, for the harvest is ripe. Come, go down; For the winepress is full, The vats overflow—For their wickedness is great" (NKJV). Christ also makes reference to this in Matthew 13:30: "Let both grow together until the harvest, and at the time of harvest, I will say to the reapers, 'First gather together the tares and bind them in bundles to burn them, but gather the wheat into my barn'" (NKJV).

Chapter 15 is the shortest chapter in the book of Revelation; it proclaims the last seven judgments on the earth. If we compare this chapter with Leviticus 26:21 we read, "If you walk contrary to Me and are not willing to obey Me, I will bring on you seven times more plagues, according to your sins" (NKJV).

This affirms God's promise of His seven final plagues.

In chapter 16, the command from heaven is given to unleash the plagues upon the earth. This also parallels Psalm 79:6, "Pour out Your wrath on the nations that do not know You, And on the kingdoms that do not call on Your name" (NKJV), and Jeremiah 10:25, "Pour out Your fury on the

Gentiles, who do not know You, And on the families who do not call on Your name" (NKJV).

It is also interesting how these plagues compare with the earlier plagues of Egypt in the book of Exodus. In Revelation 16:15, the promise from our Lord is repeated: "Behold, I am coming as a thief. Blessed is he who watches, and keeps his garments, lest he walk naked and they see his shame" (NKJV).

We also find this statement in 1 Thessalonians 5:4: "But you, brethren, are not in darkness, so that this Day should overtake you as a thief" (NKJV). (Note: it is our awesome loving Lord and Savior who keeps on reminding us of His grace. The awesome love of our Lord is always giving us the chance for redemption. Praise His name!)

This next chapter tells of the harlot (the spiritual Babylon, the religious system that corrupts the world). Verse 8 is another encouraging statement about redemption for those who are found in the book of life. We can also hear Christ in Matthew 25:34 saying, "Come, you blessed of My Father, inherit the kingdom prepared for you from the foundation of the world" (NKJV).

In reading about all of these calamities, you'll always find a verse of hope tied in.

Chapter 18 paints a picture of the physical destruction of Babylon (today's modern-day Baghdad). Within one hour Babylon is to fall. The unredeemed citizens will retch, lament and mourn over such great wealth laid to such great waste; never to rise again.

Chapter 19:9 describes the marriage supper of the Lamb: "Blessed are those who are called to the marriage supper of the Lamb!" (NKJV). Compare this with the parable in Luke 14:15–24. Notice that Christ invited all to accept His invitation, but few accepted.

In Revelation 19:11–14, the heavens open, and all behold a white horse. These verses refer to the Second Coming of Christ, when Christ returns with His Church. "Then the sign of the Son of Man will appear in heaven, and then all the tribes of the earth will mourn, and they will see the Son of Man coming on the clouds of heaven with power and great glory" (Matthew 24:30 NKJV). Then in Matthew 26:64 Christ says, "Nevertheless, I say to you, hereafter you will see the Son of Man sitting at the right hand of the Power, and coming on the clouds of heaven" (NKJV).

In chapter 20, you'll read of the millennium reign of Christ; which portrays Him sitting on David's earthly throne for 1,000 years. Throughout the testaments, promises connected to this prophecy can be found (e.g., 2 Samuel 7:12–13 and Isaiah 9:7). Luke 1:32–33 says, "He will be great and will be called the Son of the Highest; and the Lord God will give Him the throne of His father David. And He will reign over the house of Jacob forever, and of His kingdom there will be no end" (NKJV).

After 1,000 years, comes the final judgment—the lake of fire. This too was prophesied in Daniel 7:9–11 and Acts 17:31. This chapter ends with the book of Life, which is also referred to in Exodus 32:32, Psalm 69:28, Philippians 4:3 and Luke 10:20.

Now in chapter 21, the new heavens and the new earth are introduced. Looking back in Scripture, read Isaiah 65:17: "For behold, I create new heavens and a new earth; And the former all not be remembered or come to mind" (NKJV). "Nevertheless, we, according to His promise, look for new heavens and a new earth in which righteousness dwells" (2 Peter 3:13 NKJV). And of course, Matthew 6:10 says, "Thy kingdom come" (KJV).

And finally, the New Jerusalem will be revealed with all of its magnificent beauty of costly stones, gold and pearls; its radiance is sent forth from the glory of God.

And now the climax of the Bible—Revelation 22. This chapter may be summed up in one message and promise, repeated three times: "I am coming quickly" (Rev. 22:7; 22:12; 22:20 NKJV).

This message was in Isaiah 40:10 as well: "Behold, the Lord GOD shall come with a strong hand, And His arm shall rule for Him; Behold, His reward is with Him, And His work before Him" (NKJV).

 In closing, it all comes down to Christ saying in John 14:6, "I am the way, the truth, and the life. No one comes to the Father except through Me." (NKJV).

Do you know Christ personally? Does His Spirit live in your heart? To accept Christ, all you have to do is confess your sins, admit that you are a sinner and ask Christ to take residence in your heart. If you accept Him, then He will accept you. The Bible was given to us so that we could know the God who created us. We were made to glorify our maker, and in doing so we are given the promise of promises—eternal life. This promise can be summed up in the book of Revelation where Christ reveals His plans to us and then adds on the promise of everlasting life with Him, a promised reward of such immense proportions that it surpasses all of our understanding. To accept Him means the greatest of all rewards— eternally abiding in His Word and the light of His love. Remember, "If anyone has an ear, let him hear" (Rev. 13:9 NKJV).

Therefore, may all who hear or have heard His words live and follow His words. In Jesus' name I pray, Amen.

"Behold, I come quickly. Blessed is he who keeps the words of the prophecy of this book" (Rev. 22:7 WEB).

A B O U T   T H E
M I N I S T R Y

Psalms for the World, Inc., is a non-profit (501c3) ministry with a supreme desire to spread the gospel to "all the ends of the earth." We, at Psalms for the World, focus on bringing youths to Christ through a musical ministry, while providing sound biblical teaching. We focus on Southeast Asian countries, such as Bangladesh, China, Hong Kong, India, Japan, Macau, Philippines, S. Korea, Singapore, Thailand, etc. It is our desire to print our teachings in each language in which we minister.

If our ministry has touched your heart and you would like to assist in the funding of spreading the gospel to "all the ends of the earth," then a gift or pledge in any amount would be a blessing to furthering The Lord's work.

May the Lord richly bless you.

In Christ,

Psalms for the World Ministries

TESTIMONY

Greetings and blessings in the name of our Lord and Savior Jesus Christ. My name is John Mendola, and I am here to testify the grace of our Lord. I was driving to work one morning, listening to a CD, when suddenly my CD player stopped playing. The only radio station that would come in was a station that preached the gospel. I heard a testimony from a pastor (Raul Ries), speaking of the things that God has done in his life. On my way home from work, I heard my first verse-by-verse Bible study by Pastor Chuck Smith of Calvary Chapel in Costa Mesa, California. Living in Southern California, with a typical forty-five-minute commute in each direction, left me with two choices: the gospel or nothing. After two weeks of listening to these messages, I then started attending the studies and became very interested in the Bible. The Holy Spirit opened my heart and eyes to Scripture, and now my passion in life is to tell people about Jesus Christ. The Lord has used me as an instrument to preach His gospel around the world, and by His grace and power, He has blessed me through His blood. I now await the inheritance of His Kingdom and a glorious crown of victory. May the power of the Holy Spirit give you the peace and joy of our Lord and Savior Jesus Christ.

As I Remain,

John Michael Mendola

B I O G R A P H Y

Dr. John Michael Mendola (also known as Dr. Johnny) was born in the summer of 1962 in Long Island, New York. Being of Italian heritage, John was born and raised Roman Catholic. His love for music had him playing bass guitar at the local church masses. In 1994 while traveling through India, John had a vision, to donate sound systems to churches and to teach youths how to lead in worship. John then founded Psalms for the World Ministries. As the Holy Spirit has continued to work in his life, the Scriptures are daily being opened to him with new meaning, understanding and revelations that he desires to pass on to others.

At this time, John is an international Bible teacher and evangelist. Dr. Johnny has a MBA and PHD in Theology from Liberty University and his ministry consists of crusades, pastor conferences, and Bible studies throughout Asia, Europe, and the USA. As an ordained minister and founder of Psalms for the World Ministries, his focus is to bring youths to a saving knowledge in Christ by teaching verse-by-verse sound biblical doctrine, with an emphasis on the End Times. His burning passion is to assist others in growing in the knowledge of our Lord and Savior, Jesus Christ, and in accepting His eternal offer.

For further information regarding his schedule and availability for speaking engagements, you may contact him at:

John Michael Mendola
Psalms for the World Ministries, Inc. Phone: 949-565-1050
E-mail:jmendola62@gmail.com
www.psalmsfortheworld.org
WeChat: drjohnnyrock

STUDY AIDS

In Search of the Messiah: The Jesus Christ of the Old Testament (ISBN 1–931274–03–7)

The Inheritance: The book of Daniel presented as a novel (ISBN 1–931274–26–6)

Understanding the Future: An overview of Bible history, prophecy, and current events (ISBN 1–931274–07-X)

History and the Bible: A prophetic look at past and present events (ISBN 1–931274–00–2)

The Mystery of the Rapture: God's prophetic plan for the believer (ISBN 1–931274–01–0)

The Wrath of the Lamb: The last seven years of world history (ISBN 1–931274–02–9)

The Signs of the Times: An overview of Matthew 24 (ISBN 1–931274–13–4)

The Last Days: An overview of Ezekiel 38 and 39 (ISBN 1–931274–23–1)

The Unveiling: What the Bible has to say about the coming of the Antichrist (ISBN 1–931274–24-X)

Mene, Mene, Tekel, Upharsin: An overview of the book of Daniel (ISBN 1–931274–09–6)

The Divine Outline: A commentary on the book of Revelation (ISBN 1–931274–04–5)